3

Rebecca's Vest

KARL MILLER

Rebecca's Vest

A MEMOIR

HAMISH HAMILTON · LONDON

HAMISH HAMILTON LTD

Published by the Penguin Group
Penguin Books Ltd, 27 Wrights Lane, London w8 5tz, England
Penguin Books USA Inc., 375 Hudson Street, New York, New York 10014, USA
Penguin Books Australia Ltd, Ringwood, Victoria, Australia
Penguin Books Canada Ltd, 10 Alcorn Avenue, Toronto, Ontario, Canada m4v 3b2
Penguin Books (NZ) Ltd, 182–190 Wairau Road, Auckland 10, New Zealand

Penguin Books Ltd, Registered Offices: Harmondsworth, Middlesex, England

First published 1993
1 3 5 7 9 10 8 6 4 2

Grateful acknowledgement is made to the following for permission to reproduce previously
published material: Carcanet Press Ltd for lines from 'Empty Vessel' by Hugh MacDiarmid,
published in *Selected Poems* (1992); J. M. Dent Ltd for lines from 'Before I Knocked' by Dylan
Thomas, published in *Selected Poems* (1975); Faber & Faber Ltd for lines from 'The Beach
Head' and 'Tamer and Hawk' by Thom Gunn, published in *Selected Poems* (1979); the Andrew
Young Estate for lines from 'Suilven' by Andrew Young.

Typeset by Datix International Limited, Bungay, Suffolk
Printed in England by Clays Ltd, St Ives plc
Filmset in 11/13pt Garamond

A CIP catalogue record for this book is available from the British Library

ISBN 0–241–13456–0

Contents

CHAPTER ONE

When Did You First See Your Father?

Early in 1931, after a courtship of several years and a marriage of several months, my mother left my father in London and returned to their native Scotland. Concealed about her person was my person, of which she was to be light in the August of that year. My parents fell out in the course of the difficulties people faced during what used to be called – in the days when it could be thought that there had been only the one and would never be another – the Depression. My father was a landscape painter, but he can never have hoped to earn a living by painting landscapes, and it seems that there was trouble between them over what other job he might find to do, or be willing to do. From then on, each parent was to be without a partner, and my father was to become something of a recluse, carrying his easel, paints and turpentine, and a satchel of Ryvita and prunes, from one rural or suburban spot to another, many of them encountered on the glow in the neighbourhood of Wimbledon Common. Meanwhile my mother went on to fend for herself by working as an accountant in hotels and in a grocer's shop.

I was brought up near Edinburgh by my mother's mother, a widow, in a household of Connors which included three spinster aunts and an uncle. At her village school in 1880, my grandmother embroidered for a sampler the maxim:

> Be you to others kind and true
> As you'd have others be to you.

When I look at her sampler now, I am reminded of an occasion, earlier in the nineteenth century, when Thomas Carlyle scoffed at James Hogg – who kept his sheep to the south of us, in the Border hills – for appearing to say in his novel, the *Confessions of a Justified Sinner*: 'Be not angry.' Fancy writing a book to urge the Scots not to be angry, Carlyle seems to have thought, and I can just hear his angry Scots laugh. Both maxims strike me as better than most. I soon became aware that my granny was as good as her sampler's word; and I was also to learn, at a somewhat later date, that she spoke the same Scots tongue that Hogg had put, among others, in his *Confessions* – the masterpiece of literary duality, of the imagined double. 'I canna thole it,' she'd say, I can't stand it, when teased by her new child.

For the first five years of my life I barely knew where my father was or who he was. Both parents suffered the disapproval of the Connors, which was never entirely to relent. Opening her eyes in a hospital bed, after decades of not speaking and not seeing, my mother was to greet a sister with the words: 'Ye're auffy auld.' My father William was referred to in the Connor house as Miller: a manner of speaking of this alien which was to be revived in her last days, in termagant moods, by the last to die of my Connor aunts, a fourth, who lived in Fife – and directed at myself. Long durations, these.

There were Connors who felt for my father the straight arrow's scorn for the bohemian, and they may have felt that I was at risk, as I grew into my shorts and sandals, of turning into a further bohemian. Both at my village school and as I grew on into other garments I would now and then learn that various experts held that I was 'lazy' and 'dreamy'; an English aunt by marriage warmed to the theme and gave the woman I was going to marry fair warning of the slough that lay ahead. But then it was the Connors who had taken me in and looked after me, and they looked after me without making a performance of it, as if it was a natural thing – though I was enough of an unnatural thing, too, to have, when documents presented themselves for signature, not a parent, but a 'guardian': the word seemed, a little, to mark me as peculiar, wild. The family fault was to bear grudges. But it would be wrong to think of any of them as especially straight or flinty, and the toughest of my aunts was the one I got on with best in the long run.

This was Peggy, a dressmaker, whose dealings with a flighty sister were to be portrayed, as it seemed to me, in *The Dressmaker*,

Beryl Bainbridge's novel about Second World War Liverpool. Peggy's flighty sister was nice-looking, flirtatious, storytelling Betty, of the wavy blonde hair and perfect legs, a graduate and a teacher, barred from the marriage bed by sundry shadowy mischances; it can't have helped that a suitor's car door came off in her sister Jessie's hand as she advanced with her hellos, over there in Kirkcaldy, Fife. Peggy and my giddy aunt Betty were lively, interesting women who would fall into huffs with one another, in a fashion Bainbridge charts.

Peggy was the embodiment of a certain Stirlingshire maxim, a family motto: 'Haud on.' She held on, kept going, and when my grandmother died, and I was sixteen, and away in London testing the bohemian water, she became the Connor châtelaine in Gilmerton, Edinburgh. She still appears to me, as my granny does, in dreams. I once had a dream which drew me to her where she lay in a shieling in the hills, hardly more than a heap of stones. I had left the cottage for bigger things in London. She had stayed where she was, to end it among the stones.

I have also dreamt that at the age of eighty she'd become the leading scorer in the Scottish Football League, her team Heart of Midlothian – mine had once been Hibernian. My response to this news, on the pillow, was to begin writing an essay about it. Why had she not shown her skills when I was young? The next thing I knew I'd gone to see her play. She turned out in a blonde wig, to hide her age from the fans. There she was, the devil. There were the 'neat feet and legs' she'd admired in women. She had the eagle eye of Kenny Dalglish and the scuttling style of Jimmy Greaves. She scored a goal.

Half-Hibernian themselves, the Connors would sometimes disapprove of the Irish presence in Midlothian, where immigrants, such as my Connor grandfather, would frequently move from their points of arrival in the west. William Miller was Irish only in his capacity to invite severity. He was the son of a marine engineer in Glasgow, who was reputed to have played for that city's Protestant football team, Rangers. I noticed that my uncle Robert Connor was in one of the teams that fought the 1990 Scottish Cup Final, and that my father was on the bench as one of its substitutes. The names were the same, at any rate. Scotland and Ireland played together in that Aberdeen side, and the Connors and the Millers were united at last.

My first memory is of tasting a laburnum leaf while hidden in a bush in the front garden of the new house to which, on that day, my birthday, my third Second of August, the family had moved. Up in the world, from one mining village to the bungalows surrounding another. The taste of the leaf was bitter, strange: Connor buds might have rated it a Miller taste, as turpentine was to count for me as a Miller smell.

My next memory is of an incident three years later. The scene is the playground of the village school, where I am enrolling, solo. Behind me is a long queue of mothers and children. I am in the position of Cinderella in the Rossini opera: 'Who am I? I don't really know.' I am asked for my father's name. 'I think it's Tommy,' I reply. I am referring to another uncle – a simple soul, like one of his sisters, Kate, and a near relation in more senses than one: in Moredun Park Gardens I share his bed, disputing with him over the blankets. A mother in the queue intervenes to put the matter right. I was thereafter to be strangely interested in the Victorian painting which shows a noble boy under interrogation by Roundheads during the Sassenach Civil War: when did he last see his father?

We were a family of orphans or quasi-orphans, interested in sad stories. My mother spoke of her sisters as 'the hag beauties' (rather as she herself could be spoken of as my 'dear mama'), and if she was a Cinderella, so was her only son, and so were her sisters Betty and Kate and her brother Tom. 'I wish I were where Helen lies': even Peggy, no easy prey to sentiment, would sing very sweetly of Helen's fair Kirkconnell Lee, and I would sit engrossed, while still quite small. 'Night and day on me she cries,' cried Peggy. Airs and arias of love and loss, from folk-song and from the operas of Rossini and Donizetti, were to cast a spell, never broken. When the char forgives her sisters in Rossini's *Cenerentola* – 'Let kindness prevail' – I think this the song of songs. It belongs to a happy ending, but it makes a sad, indeed a tragic sound. When such music turns to the magic of good fortune, restoration and forgiveness, tuned to some notion of the glass slipper and the prince, it generally fades from my head. But when it is sad it is very, very sad, and can be a wonder of the world. It can be called, among other names, the music of self-pity, and of all those people who have a taste for grief. We love to listen to it, out here in the cold.

In and around this school playground there ensued sights and sensations which may have served to deepen my experience of an unsettling enrolment. I remember a disturbed woman of the village, her face twisted up in a mirthless grin, being followed through the streets by a crowd of jeering kids. As with my 'Civil War' interrogation, I was in due course to light on resemblances to this in the literary and artistic culture. Followed through the streets, the woman was like Madge Wildfire in Walter Scott's *Heart of Midlothian*; she was also like Robert Louis Stevenson's witch Thrawn Janet, 'thrawn' being a Scots word for stubborn and for warped. And I shall never forget, from my time at that school of warrior Prods, which would form itself into rings to witness its many boxing-matches, an Irish Catholic boy with foreign black hair and a fat red face, who had to fight and fight to protect his younger brothers from the hard men of the playground. It wasn't that I liked him, or helped him. But he was a hero. This episode, sequel to a neglected history of persecution and exploitation in the Lothians of earlier times, hasn't made me want to support the murdering IRA, but it was to teach me something about their murders.

I did not join in the disapproval of my parents which could be voiced in the house, though never by my grandmother. I didn't feel like blaming, or worshipping, an absent father. Occasionally I'd fancy some male or other in the role of surrogate: when war broke out, I travelled in a bus examining a soldier, beneath whose absorbing forage cap was a possible dad. With my mother I remained in touch, and would eventually cycle over to argue with her, on Sunday afternoons, where she lived in the lee of the Pentland Hills. The time came when we'd go to the pictures – foreign pictures, imported by a film society, with a love interest which was to be of mounting concern to the person in the black school blazer and matching cap, who then began to dress for the occasion, *à la bohème* – a blame come true – in exotic turtleneck sweater and chocolate corduroy jacket. Oh my Mai Zetterling and my Arletty. And oh my mother, there beside me in the stalls of the Caledonian Cinema, looking up a little grimly at the tumbles on the screen.

During the previous world war my father was, like my friend on the bus, a soldier. He served in the Argyll and Sutherland Highlanders, and was captured in a Flanders shell hole and sent to Germany, where he was well treated by a farmer for whom he worked. I believe that I am called after that farmer, though it was also to be rumoured that I was called after Karl Marx, having narrowly missed commemorating George Bernard Shaw.

I have never been conscious of bearing my parents any ill-will for not being around. I used to reckon that I understood how they had come to part, and to part from me. It became possible to think of their involvement as a love story, to think that the attachment hadn't altogether been spoiled by anger and rashness, and by the way of the world. But perhaps it had. Late in their lives I met William as he descended a London staircase with his satchel of healthy foods – maybe I'd been hoping to promote a reunion in the flat above – and was saluted with a coarse inquiry as to the identity of the old woman upstairs. Scottish readers will grasp that this was a joke, and that, as with my mother's words in the hospital bed, the abrasive question may have secreted some affection.

'Half an hour of him is as much as I can take.' This was another joke – my mother's this time, on the same occasion. It referred to me, the interceder. As I remember it, my father let me know that she had made the remark during this (fruitless) interview, shortly before I began toiling up the stairs. It may be that I am sewing together, for my sampler, jokes made on separate occasions. If so, they may be said to be jokes that belong together, snubs that snuggle up, occasions that conspire. I find them funny, and there's a certain exhilaration in the rejections they transmit.

A struggle began inside me between the example set by my father and that of my Uncle Bob, who had gone down the pit at the age of fifteen and emerged to become a grey eminence in electrical engineering, who lived in Manchester, was awarded the Order of the British Empire for wartime services, and would draw up in a car during the war, tired and ministerially remote, at the foot of our garden path. The diary I had started to keep described the visits paid by my uncle and his formidable English wife, Ida, in earlier days a singer of opera and oratorio. I mentioned his 'air of frigid Olympian quiet', 'the awe of their presence'. They were a bit like kings and queens, or like gods who had come down to earth to see how we were getting on, or holding on. Their visits disclosed a high ground somewhere else, where human beings were grave and important. I may have been trying to be like him when many years later I enrolled for a spell of service, dark-suited, in the Treasury, down the street from the office in Victoria where I'd found him once, after lunch, dictating letters and smoking a cigar.

For the most part, though, it pleased me to think of myself as the son of an artist and professed anarchist and of a socialist mother. A parcel of books arrived from my father in London, books which were worried over in Edinburgh as perhaps subversive but which scarcely amounted to a bomb: one of them was Matthew Arnold's *Culture and Anarchy*. At this time he was earning his living in a commercial-art studio near Fleet Street, and his visits to Gilmerton were few and far between. I recall a treat, a session in a tearoom, where I am eyeing some sweet thing which his in-laws say is not good for me. My father objects that if you don't like something it's unlikely to be good for you. That sank in, as a foreign sentiment that made sense. I was not to know that Edinburgh's gutta-percha wartime-austerity cakes, with their bulbs of rubber cream, were about as wholesome as bombs.

I visited him after the war in London, where he was working as a Post Office clerk at Mount Pleasant, a sorter of telegrams, and when I married and a child was born I was visited at my house in London, every week or so, by the hermit. The hermit remarked that he was a late developer, unlike me, and that he was a hermit, not cut out for family life. But he played with my son to the manner born. I was virtually grown up by the time we got to know each other, and our first encounters were wary ones. There were never to be any displays of affection, any tender touches. This was not really to be expected, and there was certainly a shy friendliness in the offer of points of view in his letters, and in their deference to the views of the early developer. I don't remember embracing, or being embraced by, my mother either. Neither of them had escaped, in any comprehensive way, from a time and place where tenderness was classed with the sweet things that might not be good for you: I came in my teens to think of this time and place as an Old World that had been checked and maybe superseded by modern love and modern poetry. But then again, I remember planting plenty of kisses on the soft sea-sand wrinkles of my grandmother's ivory cheeks and pulling at her old tholing ears.

When I first saw my father in London he was living in his customary rather gruelling austerity, with its traces of military hardship, a sourness as of wars and depressions, in the attic of a house in King's Cross, in Calthorpe Street, which I often walk along now, and never without responding to the note which the name has sounded for me since the days when I used to study it on letters. He set himself to paint my portrait in this attic, until I got on his nerves with my fidgeting. My son Daniel, who is a painter too, and who was to undergo his own passage of King's Cross austerity, once laughed at me for 'tussling' with him at the kitchen sink over some dish-washing matter; on the other occasion I tussled with my father at the easel, and he landed a few mild blows. I seem to have stalked my parents through London, as if I were trying to catch up. At one point I discovered that I had lived for years in a street in Chelsea where my mother had had a room. I would like, for circularity's sake, to think that this was the scene of the primal rift.

My father remained in some degree strange to me, but I sympathised with his intransigence, and with his green pictures. He went to Glasgow Art School, but he never exhibited, and probably never tried to, and is unlikely ever to have met a dealer. He had no time for 'abstractionists', and we were soon to disagree about modern art, and in particular about Picasso, of whom he was given to speaking in offended terms. His own pictures spoke of Pissarro, and of the light that falls on a cold land. His suns shone down from promising blue skies on grasses, leaves, the black pillars of his trees, patches of park, of tawny scrub, beige bits of path and bank (his sisters-in-law were sufficiently fond of that last colour to pronounce a relative's coffin 'a beautiful shade of beige'). He was devoted to such sights, and to peaceful, seemingly untenanted suburban houses, in a London that could still be green and rural.

Going through his papers after his death, I happened on a passage – copied out in his handwriting – which had to do with three grounded telegraph poles:

> To the left the sun is in the act of rising. Each pole has its attendant shadow, four or five feet wide, and the old wheel tracks in the grass, almost invisible at mid-day, are like canyons full of blue darkness. As a 'view', nothing could be more perfectly pointless; and yet, for some reason, it contains all beauty, all significance, the subject-matter of all poetry.

What could this be? When could this be? I later came across the passage in Aldous Huxley's *Time Must Have a Stop*, which I had first read in 1947 – possibly at my father's suggestion – two years after the novel was published.

It is from an item in the notebooks of the hero, Sebastian Barnack, characterised by the publisher of a paperback reissue as 'a young man with the beauty of an angel, the creative power of a great artist and the tiresomeness of a spoilt child', whose eyes are opened to earthly delights when he arrives in Florence to stay with a hedonistic uncle, and then, with the war giving way to peace and with time giving way to eternity, to heavenly ones. Out, at this point, come Sebastian's notebooks. What he says here about the view from the window of his 'inn' was bound to have appealed to my father. The view from that window is like one of his pictures.

My reverent father went after such sights whenever he could, and there was no difficulty in recognising an aspect of him in Joyce Cary's portrait of an artist, *The Horse's Mouth*. But I was to prefer him to Cary's boorish genius – 'utterly disregardful of outrageous fortune and social carefulness', as the young Philip Larkin was to note. Larkin 'liked the idea of the mad old bastard going to jail and stealing snuffboxes . . . and painting away on that garage wall while the Council demolish it'. When William Miller wasn't painting or walking or earning, he read books; and this anarchist read the *Daily Telegraph* for the news it had in it. Both parents, four hundred miles apart, devoured Dostoevsky. My mother was the greater reader of the two: she mispronounced Proust's name, but she read what he had written. She had no feeling, however, for the painted word. My father was to offer me a quotation from Nietzsche: 'When you go among women, don't forget your whip.' His whip? This was a joke, or half-joke, as well, perhaps, as a forlorn vaunt in the Northern style.

The tribes to the north and west of Hadrian's Wall, not least when they came to gather themselves into cities, have been quarrelsome and fierce, and anxious to appear so. The behaviour of the Connors and Millers was to enhance such appearances, to add to the collective threat. But it should also be said that some part of the hostility of the tribes in question, as we know it now, is a show, a joke, a boast, and a confession of weakness. My mother used to do a little turn, an imitation of James Cagney, squaring up in his trenchcoat and saying: 'You dirty rat.' The turn made me think of my father, who looked faintly like the gangster star: but by one man who was his friend in London, and who referred to him as Jock, he was thought gentle. Neither parent was free from the phobias of tribe and race, and my mother was successively drawn to Hitler and to Stalin: no politician was all bad who threatened a retribution on Churchill and the Duke of Edinburgh. There was more anger in her than there was in him, and much more humour. Marion was the right name for her, said Minnie, as she was usually known, in view of the adage: 'Marry in haste, repent at leisure.' For her, it had been the other way round.

She was fair and he was dark. She had full lips and long legs, with feet that turned outwards to right and left, as if to keep pace with those punishing foreigners of hers. I did not look like my father, who was slight and lean, with aquiline features, fierce and yet not fierce; a hazelnut-shell cast of fingernail was among the few points we shared. I was growing up to prefer dark looks to a native mousiness. At the same time, his strange appearance may have helped to hold me back from him. I now prize being there, being with, as mattering more than blood relationship, fingernails, physical and legal affinity. But resemblance has continued to claim me. When I went to Ireland, I marvelled at the sameness of its persons, at the spectacle of Dublin's Dublin faces, in which I also caught glimpses of my own.

My father visited me when I was a student at Cambridge, and we parted after a quarrel. Having then gone off into the countryside to paint, gentle Jock was arrested for looking like a murderer whom the police were seeking. During the second war, when he was in the Fire Service, he had wandered off without leave to paint in some other countryside, and been sent to jail, like Cary's Gulley Jimson. He afterwards elected to do time at a lay monastery in Shropshire. This Anglo-German Society of Brothers dated from before the war and consisted of Christians who believed that 'individualism' had caused the world to go wrong and that toil and soil were the answer.

He became ill in the Sixties, having made clear, in the past, his aversion to any struggle with sickness which kept him from his trees and grasses: on a previous visit to a hospital he had taken with him a knife – to stab himself with it if the news was bad. A moment of fame befell him at White Hart Lane football ground, where I was fetched from the crowd by an announcement on the public-address system and dispatched to the Battersea morgue. I was driven from the ground by my Irish-faced friend Danny Blanchflower, a well-known footballer allergic to the intrusions of fame. The face I stared at in the morgue was as if struck or swept away – the prediction of a traumatic self-portrait done by my son Daniel. An inquest found that my father had been poisoned by the fumes from a gas-ring beside which he was sitting, perhaps for warmth. Like the castaway in William Cowper's poem of that name, he 'drank the stifling wave, and then he sank.'

His estranged wife died a number of years later. She'd taken, latterly, to imagining threats, hearing voices, a habit that was to be aggravated by the drugs they give to the old. I gathered from her that her room was wired to receive radio messages from book reviewers in corrupt London, one or two of whom, associates of mine, she had identified, on stylistic grounds, as me. She'd earlier imagined that the romantic poet George Barker was an agent of the Pope. A voice of my own tells me that she wasn't altogether wrong about that. None of her messages was dull.

'I think it is not too good to be dependent on other people. I am the awful example of the other extreme.' This is my father speaking, and these words, too, must have sunk in. They could well have reminded me of another example of the extreme, that of another miller, the jolly one who lived and sang by the River Dee:

> I care for nobody, no, not I,
> And nobody cares for me.

An eminent man was informed by a companion not long ago that a great institutional post had gone to someone or other, and that the companion did not know this someone. 'Indeed!' screamed the eminent man. '*Nobody* knows him!' And in *Tom Jones* Henry Fielding writes tongue-in-cheek about the 'scandal' of 'being one whom nobody knows', a scandal 'as old as Homer'. And as recent as William Miller. It soon made sense to think of him as a man whom nobody knew and who knew that he would never be known, and to think of him, in certain moods, as one of the exemplary poor, practically an ascetic. The scandal of William Miller was something in which I could take pride, as I awoke to the business of interpreting how he stood in the world. He was plainly not eminent. There were traits, such as the newspaper he read and the sports jacket he wore, which might have seemed middle-class: other traits, however, suggested bare subsistence and the hair shirt. He regarded himself as having suffered from 'poor man's gout'. After rising in the world, I was to suffer myself from the other kind. *Chacun à sa goutte.* I also appear to suffer from my mother's sense of humour.

There can't be many who are truly indifferent to indifference, and it just isn't in most artists, surely, not to mind an indifference to their art; and it's no less the case that art takes advantage of the audience it obtains, if it obtains one, and collaborates with it. My father had to manage without such advantages, without attention and without connections, and he did manage – while quite often giving the impression that there was no managing to do, that he was camped on that fortunate island where art and status are ignorant of each other and no one has to overcome neglect. He did not complain, and he went on with his art to the end. I liked that in him, and I disliked and feared the filial converse in myself – a dependence on others and on the opinion of others. It wasn't that I felt that I should become a tramp or a monk when I grew up. But the thought of what it was to be 'alienated' cast a juvenile spell.

He lived with his lack of consequence at a time when conse-quence grew more consequential, importance more important. His earlier life had been darkened by war and unemployment: the spartan state of his garrets, the newspapers spread as dust-covers on the armchairs where he never sat, the pound notes stowed in cupboards, were an acknowledgement of this. The world he looked at must have seemed to be one in which a pursuit of survival had been followed by a pursuit of success, and there was a world on the way in which more people than before would be forced to think themselves failures, in which their country could itself be thought to have failed, but in which fame and fortune had moved to the top of the national curricu-lum, and in which an artist's success would come about when his name was in the papers, and when his prospects had become futures, his paintings a portfolio of investments.

From the days of my infant staggerings-off into the country-side I have been inclined to think in terms of separations and stays, and to wonder about my father's way of life, to be impressed by it and warned by it. I was to join in and join up, but have often seen myself as due both to run away and to be shut out. As an evacuee during the war, at the age of eight, I pined for home and sat in my bath nibbling a bar of soap, in a less than Roman attempt to end it all. Like the laburnum leaf, the soap tasted strange, and a shade deathly. But I did not die. My mother complained, mistakenly, that I was being ill-treated by the couple who had taken me in, and, to my great, maybe my first embarrassment, I was transferred to another house. Shortly afterwards I was off down the road to Edinburgh, back to my grandmother and to my Aunt Peggy, who was in her last days to make much the same journey when she fled from an old people's home in the country. Having reached Moredun Park, I took part with my womenfolk in a contemplative pause next to the laburnum bush, before being returned to rural Penicuik, on which the Germans then flew in and dropped a bomb.

When I was young, I wanted, in a Scottish way, to get on, and eventually inquired into the question of a possible link between the desire to do well in the eyes of others, to be well-known for that, or at any rate for something, and a denial of affection experienced or invented in early life. An essay by Robert Hughes on the paintings of Frank Auerbach relays the semi-orphan Thomas De Quincey's suggestion that 'it is, or it is not, according to the nature of men, an advantage to be orphaned at an early age.' It seems like a guarded suggestion: but Hughes obligingly points out that loss can be a 'creative goad'. It is just as plain, or it is no less obscure, that loss can also lead to refusals and flights, or worse, in the field of the affections. There may have been a bit of this in the case of my father, whose mother was reported to have been generally somehow hostile, and who was never to speak to me about his parents.

There were to be times when people have wanted me out. This happens to nearly everyone, poor things. When it has happened to me it has happened to a self-imagined seasoned abstainer who was none the less capable of surprise at the notice to quit: it doesn't do to suppose that they might not want you to leave. But I went on with my relish for leaving, and even for exclusion. The other evening I was ordered by my grandson to 'go out' of the room, and the door was then firmly shut by the little man. I was thrilled. 'This,' I whispered to myself, 'is where I came in.'

Getting married young and having children was to recondition the adolescent egotist I am describing in this book. I was to be less of the kind of leaver who actually clears off. I had been warned by the example of my parents' separate ways. But there was no need for me to be warned to take pleasure in spending time with my family. This did not mean that they were never to be troubled by persistences of mine in the orphan mode.

To the extent of my consciousness that my parents had let me go and that I had been 'taken in', I was a foster child. By and large, however, and not only by foundling standards, I was fortunate; I even came to believe in luck, and to believe that I had had my share, while remaining suspicious of happy endings. I was not denied affection. I rated low on the Barnardo's scale. My childhood was such that when I hear now of challenges by sires and dams over children who have been looked after by others, I feel for the adoptive parents. And yet an orphan self took hold: vulnerable and fierce, bereaved and aggrieved. It came and it went; in time, it was to be tempered and concealed, rather than outgrown.

To the extent of its hold, I was persuaded that my role was to suffer – a persuasion that survived the discovery that many people with mothers and fathers and brothers and sisters to be with, and to complain of, felt the same way. The books that I began to read proved to be full of the persuasion, and of the individual self-interest that inspires it. So I was not alone in being alone. Literature was my friend, and so was the diary I began to keep, in which this self, at its most unrestrained, was written down. It was far from identical, I would guess, with the human being visible to those around me, and it is now comic and painful to me in the rewriting; even at the time, I could see the joke. This is a book about the first twenty-five years of my life, with a few forward marches to the present tense of my last days, and a descent into the seventeenth century, for a visit to a man who once lived where I did, and did what I did. It is an attempt to speak of adolescent self-pity, of adolescent discontents, and of their location in a cultural scene.

CHAPTER TWO

Heart of Midlothian

The village of Straiton, where I saw the light, was so called, in all modesty, as a place through which a person might pass at speed on the way to some other place – straight on to Penicuik in particular. It stood at the foot of the south-eastern slopes of the benevolent blue Pentland Hills, from which, in wintertime, stricken deer would descend for human help, their eyes closed with ice. 'I to the hills will lift mine eyes' – it was of the Pentlands that the Psalm was always to make me think. My own person was soon borne, together with our chattels, down to the outskirts of Edinburgh, where bungalows were going up, cement-mixers turning, and where there were to be lairs for children in the half-built houses, pharaonic chambers, where their rebellious cigarettes would presently be lit.

On the way down, just outside Straiton, our chattels would have skirted 'Jeanie Deans' wood'. Jeanie is the 'plain, true-hearted, honest' heroine of Walter Scott's novel *Heart of Midlothian*, who walks and hitches to London to plead with the Queen on behalf of her flighty sister Effie, who has been sentenced to death for the alleged murder of her illegitimate child. Jeanie has also conscientiously refused to bear false witness in her sister's favour. She can't for the life of her tell a lie in order to save the life of the 'castaway': a moving dilemma, more moving than what happens next, when unromantic Jeanie, as Scott supposes her, Cinderellas it to the ball in London. 'I have that within me,' she says, 'that will keep my heart from failing.' For Louisa Stuart, Scott's friend (and mine, when I came to read her and to write about her), she was a rare specimen of virtue made endearing in fiction. By John Buchan Effie is ineffably described as 'true woman, the passionate spoiled beauty, with the good breeding which in any class may accompany bodily loveliness'. Tradition had it, in my day, that Jeanie washed her feet in that wood at the start of her journey, but the novel, which should know, does not say so, and I take it that the wood is no more hers than was the humble dwelling – at the foot of Edinburgh's little mountain, Arthur's Seat – which was photographed in the later years of the last century as 'Jeanie Deans''. And yet she is fact as well as fiction. Real places were named after her. She had an original in the aptly-named Helen Walker of Irongray in the South-West of Scotland, who went to London on a similar and equally successful mission of clemency. And she has been an incarnation of Scottish worth, puritanism's human face and best foot forward, with real people striving to resemble her.

Jeanie and Effie romantically reminded me of my aunts Peggy and Betty, and Jeanie's journey supplied me with a pattern for momentous transfers of the person from Edinburgh to London and from London to Edinburgh: my own and my Uncle Bob's, Ben Jonson's, that of the Samuel Johnson who declared the road to England to be 'the Scotsman's noblest prospect', and many more. An early sense of the fact and fiction of Jeanie Deans was to contribute to a way of thinking, which was two ways. What I read in books – and dreamt in dreams – and what I experienced beyond books in the waking world were thereafter, on many occasions, to be jointly remembered: which was which could become a question. Literature would often be perceived as separate, a rival place of profound appeal, a place of escape: but it would also be judged to belong to the real life of the reader, working him up just as life does – to belong to a reality compounded of aims and aberrations, calculation and emotion, truth and fantasy, information and reflection.

Midlothian, as Scott puts it in the novel, marched with the Merse – through which, in Berwickshire, on the far side of the Lammermuir Hills, flowed the River Tweed. For hundreds of years both regions have been inhabited by writers, and are in some degree determined by their writings. Jeanie Deans' wood, and Helen Walker's name, gave evidence of the liveliness and life-shaping properties of literature and of language, as did the Eildon Hills, split in three by the magic of a wizard's imagination, that of the thirteenth-century astrologer Michael Scott, and lived near, in baronial guise, by another wizard, another Scott, whose bedizened Madge Wildfire was later to seem to have some sisterly connection with a Madam Doubtfire known to me in Edinburgh, a seller of old clothes, having already resembled my village victim. There within me, for real, was this book about imaginary Jeanie by your actual Walter Scott, which I came to know before I came to read it, and in which I read that the Heart of Midlothian was the name for a jail.

We were now settled in our new house, downhill towards Edinburgh from this village of Gilmerton. The day came when I made love to my mother earth. A group of small boys, Just Williams and Oor Wullies, is standing about. Some thinker has persuaded us to hump the ground, and a wee hole has been dug for the purpose. One by one, oor wullies are lowered into the space, and we perform our urchin thrusts. The earth does not move.

No small girls were present at the rite. But small girls were abroad in Moredun Park Gardens, and they were our friends and equals, though set somewhat apart from us. On a later occasion I joined a row of boys outside a hut where building materials were stored. In the shadowy inside of the hut, like an idol in a shrine of cement bags, was a vague, fair, freckled older lassie. When my turn came, I went in to place a kiss on her freckles and to lift up a solemn hand to her soft scone breasts.

On a hill over to the right of Moredun Park, as you faced north to the city, were the ruins of Craigmillar Castle, where doomed Mary Queen of Scots, a favourite female of my youth, had sometimes stayed, and where marmalade was said, it would seem incorrectly, to have been invented for her when she was ill and named after her. At the foot of the hill were some cottages, called Little France after those of her foreign retainers who had lived there, and an oak tree planted by her and reduced to tatters by relic-seekers such as myself. Nearby was a wood, widdled through by a burn, where we pretended to be Mohicans. We found German steel helmets which were really po's or pudding basins, and treasure chests which were never to budge from the bowels of mother earth.

Over the hill from beyond the castle would once in a while swarm Iroquois braves, raiding parties from a grim enemy housing estate: the 'Craigmillar yins', we called them, fearing them as dangerous dead-enders. With these ones, scraps and stand-offs would take place. Craigmillar is reported now to be racked with drug addiction and Aids.

My first employer in journalism, Ian Gilmour, has been ennobled and has taken the name of Lord Gilmour of Craigmillar. His father inhabited a country house not far from my widdling wood, but I was unaware when I joined the *Spectator* that I'd narrowly missed being his peasant, on that other sort of estate. He knows that there is more to his fief than Mary Queen of Scots, whose castle he owns. I feel that it is my castle too.

There were wheatfields where we lived, into which, during the second war, soldiers and their girls would disappear. When, in another country place, police arrived to put a stop to such disappearances, whole Birnam Woods of lovers would rise up in their blades of grass and bits of straw and troop back to Dunsinane. On the eve of the war, there stood at the foot of the Gardens, in its shed, an aeroplane built by a local man. I don't believe it was ever to fly.

This was a storied countryside which gave onto others, as I have said. Not all of the stories were by Walter Scott, or about Scott, but many of them were. 'Was the country named after him?' I seem to hear myself ask at the age of whenever, and it has since been claimed that he invented it, trapping it in tartans, and so on. He informed a no doubt bemused Czar of Russia that as a volunteer dragoon he had engaged in 'some slight actions' such as 'the affair of Moredoun Mill'. A joke fit for a Czar's ear, had it been a little easier to understand. The Moredun enemy would have been the riotous poor, under the contagion, perhaps, of French Revolutionary principles. So keen was Scott on hierarchy that he was quick to spot it even in the tumults of rebellion: in *Heart of Midlothian* he refers, and defers, to 'the principal rioters', one of whom gets to be a baronet.

His bride of Lammermuir met her sad fate in the hills to the south: I soon learnt about that, and must have listened on the radio to the music she'd become. Donizetti's trills and swoops and sobs, dolours and plangencies and martial glooms, take me back to my first preoccupation with love and loss, sex and violence, braw lads and bonny lassies and bitter ends, and with the cherishing and exacerbation of such themes in displays of grief. The actions commemorated in the old ballads of the Border hinterland were not slight, and the ballads are great works, which Scott helped to recover. I still have strains of this minstrelsy by heart.

> I leant my back until an aik,
> I thocht it was a trusty tree.
> But first it bent and syne it brak.
> Sae my true love did lichtlie me.

A commemoration of my neighbourhood, as it was at this time, has come about in Bill Douglas's *My Childhood*, one of three autobiographical films. It is set in Newcraighall, the next village to mine towards the sea: like mine, a village of miners, and, in Douglas's film, of two deserted boys, their guardian a desolate grandmother. A deserted mother is off in a mental home, and the autobiographer is befriended by an Italian prisoner of war. The film is bleaker than anything I knew a few fields away; it displays a slow-paced cherishing virtuosity of suffering. But there is nothing in it that I can't credit. Does it exaggerate? If it does, its exaggerations are like some of my own of the same time, and it isn't as if there aren't at all times childhoods as bad as this, from which there may be no escape, no moving on to make films on the subject. Here, at any rate, coloured black, is the hard heart of Midlothian, Midlothian the prison.

There was always the lassies, as Robert Burns used to point out. One of these, though, was less a lassie than the Gardens leading lady, already a star, and a daunter of romantic feelings. A round, rather cross white face, with round blue eyes that seemed to be about to start out at you on stalks. It was as if Anne Crosbie and her parents were English, so special did they seem. Lessons in music and drama, in elocution, were heard of.

A cigarette fuming away in period style at her lips, her mother went about with her hair captured in an exotic bandana. On winter evenings the children of the street held their parliaments in the foggy light of a lamp-post at the turn of a corner, breaking off to go and listen to Tommy Handley's *ITMA* on the wireless. These were sessions which Queen Anne would seldom arrive in her coach to attend, and there was to be a daylight hour when she and the Commons had a row. 'I'll go straight to the police,' she cried in a carrying voice. 'You can go squint to the police,' I said, 'for all we care.' She was not amused by this laboured sally, but she did not go to the police. Instead she took the road to London and went on the stage, where Annette Crosbie has long been an actor's actress of notable skill. When I watch her playing her parts on television – patient Griseldas, the unamused Queen Victoria and the rest – I wish I could unsay my sally. I secretly admired her at the time, in her aloofness, and have since been visited by thoughts of how this star was born and made – with the mettle of a Jeanie Deans – in Moredun Park.

Elocution was an interest which was not confined to the Crosbies. It meant being taught to speak with a 'standard', a 'cultured', English accent. You could also teach yourself to be well-spoken-of for being, in this sense, 'well-spoken'. Many Scots who moved south were sooner or later to tune their note to the speech around them, and in Scotland itself forked tongues were and are common enough. When I started broadcasting I was advised to moderate my Scots accent, and I remember wrestling in the studio with 'palm tree'. I still have trouble saying 'father'. In the Scottish countryside I am thought to be English, and in England I am thought to be Scots, especially when night falls and I get excited.

There lived in Midlothian, in those days, a certain sensitive man with pale, ringed fingers, a lonely cissie or Jessie, who was to be caught up in this learning process. He played the piano and gave lessons, in his brown suit, and at one point he took the road to London to be interviewed for a diploma in elocution. He went by bus and by night, which at that time entailed a long wandering way down through the shires, with stops in the occasional wilderness for pees and teas. At one such stop he fell into a pond. Caked and dishevelled, he arrived near Regent's Park to face a panel of courteous English-speaking gentlemen, who inquired if there was any contemporary writer he particularly respected. He was equal to that. 'T. S. Eliot,' he replied. What poems or passages did he feel like mentioning by way of explanation? A pause ensued, which he was unable to bring to an end. 'I had to be helped out,' he told Betty Connor afterwards. 'Heavens,' cried my aunt, imagining some physical collapse.

After the mysterious, Eleusinian rituals of its early days my role as a lover of women was not resumed for a number of years, and when it was resumed the auspices were Presbyterian. For a brief while I was a religious zealot. I wasn't pressed into this by any preceptor: the Church of Scotland had lapsed by then from the more intimidating doctrines of Calvinism, and was proceeding towards an Anglican blandness, though brisk residues of the old severities and embargoes remained a prime feature of Midlothian mentalities. I would set off for Liberton Kirk dressed to the nines in the handsome navy-blue overcoat and bonnet made for me, to my embarrassment, by Peggy, squeezing the bonnet into my coat pocket as soon as I left the house. My devotions were due to be sweetened by a walk back with a girl whose portrait I painted in watercolour, stretched out on the floor beside the furious churning of Peggy's sewing-machine; next door in the sitting-room, the spent, unravelled wooden cotton-reels with which I was in the habit of staging war-games – while occasionally getting up to smoke brown-paper cigars, conduct orchestras, and deliver sermons over the back of armchairs – had yet to be laid to rest. This affair existed largely in my head: but then I was already becoming – in the words used by the boxing promoter Mickey Duff of one of his rivals – 'a legend in my own mind', and in that legend girls were now to prove, together with books, of vital importance. Looking at my stamp album, a girl from the neighbourhood spied, practically microscopic on a Spanish specimen, Goya's *Naked Maja*. She was amused, and I was disquieted. Our eyes met. The plot thickened. Something was up.

Inching towards carnality, I later made friends with a big fair-haired girl from the town, of Scandinavian stock, whose long pink legs dangled before me as we clambered through the rafters of the half-built bungalows. This friendship caused my maiden aunts to fear that I might be on the road to Bohemia, and so I was. On that road lay Portobello Swimming-Pool, where my fair friend would stand up broad-shouldered in her black one-piece costume before plunging in to execute her Viking strokes. I found that I was not aquatic; I always seemed to be trying to hoist myself over the rim of the pool in order to get out. But I was fascinated by this palace of Californian blue skies, dins and yells, splashes and sparkles, mucus and verruca, pees silent as in 'swim'. 'The sexual intercourse of things' – a pioneering expression of James Hogg's, in one of his parodies of the Lake school, for the world's blends and bonds and mucous mutualities – was tremendously in evidence. The Wordsworthism achieved by Hogg on this occasion is a poem in itself:

> The boy was stunned – for on similitude
> In dissimilitude, man's sole delight,
> And all the sexual intercourse of things,
> Do most supremely hang.

I was that very boy – stunned by Portobello's similes and slippery conjunctions.

For my Jenny Wren Aunt Peggy, Portobello Pool, now gone, was as the Baths of Caracalla in awful ancient Rome. She pointed her needle at the pool. But it has an important place in the stories that some people have chosen to tell of themselves, and of Proustian past times, of how the film star Sean Connery was once a lifeguard there. It was present in the nightmares, and is present in the memoirs, of my wonderfully ironic friend, the jazz clarinettist Sandy Brown, and Candia McWilliam has a story about a visit to the pool by a sad, bookish, ambitious miss and her girlfriend, the Swiss rolls of their towel and costume tucked beneath their Scottish oxters. A sign says 'No Petting', and the freckled narrator eyes the behaviour of the bolder spirits. A boy calls to a pretty, tanned girl, 'in a yearning voice': 'You're right stupid, that you are.' It's a precisely observant story. It has, to the life, my Peggy's slow turning-away of the head during a coldness, the eyes lingering on me, to the side of the socket, in disdain: 'The girls made much play of ignoring the boys, and when the boys looked away the girls redrew their eyes with particularly ostentatious displays of indifference.' Bobbing about in the pool, unnoticed by the author thirty years later, are yearning me and my Viking friend. At the end of the story the two well-spoken girls are accosted by a crone smelling 'of pee and dirt and drink'. This, too, is a matter of observation.

In 1943 I began to attend the Royal High School of Edinburgh, on a scholarship. The school song said that the place was like a citadel set on a hill – half-way up the Calton Hill, to be precise. The school motto said that the state depends for its flourishing on the muses. These statements were made in Latin, and it was a school where Latin and Greek were taught. Founded in the Middle Ages, it was originally the Town School. The building I went to, a late accession to the New Town, belongs to the 1820s: it is an imitation of the Temple of Theseus in Athens, and is expected to house the Scottish parliament if, as some Scots keep hoping, devolution or separation takes place. It looks out across a valley at the ridge occupied by the Old Town, where the High Street is, and the Heart of Midlothian – a heart traced out in cobbles at the spot where Scott's Tolbooth prison used to stand; here you may wish a wish, as I have never failed to do, and seal it with a spit. The boys, or 'gytes', as they were once known, wore black uniforms, switching to white for cricket and for public performances by the choir. All this was a further rise in the world, a world in which there was one set of sports for the rich – not that these pupils were all that royal and high – and another for the poor: but it was also a fall, when my soccer action ran into ignominy on the rugby field, from which I was soon to retire.

My early years at the Temple of Theseus were spent coping with the intensities of memory work and competitive study which were thought to ensure a secondary education. In some subjects the early developer proved to be a slow learner. On dark days and in drizzles the school had a mausoleum look; below the dignified pillars and pediment at the front lurked a sunless slum known as 'the dungeons', where dungs descended in Stygian stalls and the talismanic, transgressive period cigarette was smoked. For the most part, though, this piece of ancient Greece was a friendly environment, when you were used to it, full of character and of characters, both among the boys and among the masters. The boys neither bullied nor fought one another; the worst of them was the pandemonium of the lone classroom in which some vulnerable teacher was baited and overwhelmed. Condoms, flung by Romeo and Juliet from the height above, would be found sprawling in the playground on Monday mornings. Tended by the janitor, chickens hatched beneath the windows of the Geography Room, and went sprinting like schoolboys round their wire-netting cantonment; one of their dashes still lives inside me.

It was something of a literary school, with a number of learned teachers and a long history of publication. The seventeenth-century Midlothian poet William Drummond of Hawthornden, who spent his life near my birthplace of Straiton, went to the school in the days when it was sited over by the High Street, and so did Walter Scott, and Henry Mackenzie, author of *The Man of Feeling*. Co-authors, these three, among others, of the romantic sensibility. And three of the most accomplished Scottish poets of the present century had also attended the school. My own concern with this sort of thing jumped into the air from the runway on Calton Hill, and there were other boys at the school who shared the concern. Others again, Sandy Brown for one, wanted to be, and became, jazz musicians. Either way, as best we could, us chickens took wing.

On 29 November 1946, fifteen years old, I wrote: 'This day marks the opening of a journal which I hope to continue for as long as possible. Whether this book is being put to a better use than that of Homeric vocabulary, I do not know. Its purpose is to obtain an interesting evening in the future when I shall open the journal and see inscribed therein the strange workings of the adolescent mind.' Facing the first page of the journal was pasted a photograph of Bernard Shaw, emerging with an authorial frown from his writing-hut, dressed in plus-fours and wearing a pair of brogues with protruding fringed tongues. A similar pair was presently to appear on my own two feet.

I was set going as a diarist by *The Book of Maggie Owen*, the journal of an Irish orphan, started on 24 January 1908 and recently published. 'I am a virgin twelve years of age,' Maggie explains, if there really was a Maggie, for the text can convey the sense of a ghost – a reader, perhaps, of Daisy Ashford's *The Young Visiters*, which came out in 1919. 'I shall put down me best thoughts and all important things that happen to me – if any do.' Maggie's is a more engaging book than mine was ever to be, but there are certain resemblances. 'I resolve to be a noble woman but tis hard to be noble in a house along with people not noble. They dont want to be noble and hinder me spiritual efforts with teasing.' My own diary went on in several volumes for nine years. Looked at, as anticipated, in the future, the workings of the adolescent mind seem a good deal more representative than strange. It is the diary of a self-seen outcast, and is often wretchedly self-engrossed. It reviews the books I read. It contains troubles and complaints and confessions, poems and stories and girls, earnest bookish friendships with older males. It hurriedly records a series of crises, elations and longueurs.

The following February I was seized with an anxiety in which there seemed to figure various awakenings and guilts, and the battle for marks at school. Thoughts of suicide, not very oppressive ones, entered my journal. An aunt had warned me that there was 'something coming to me' – for my badness, for Portobello Pool, for the misdemeanours congregating in a diary more or less impossible to hide in a small house. Would I be asked to leave? I did not appreciate quite how much the people of Scotland are given to feeling that there is something coming to them, and to others, who are exposed, on balance, to an even greater risk of being shown up, found out, judged, damned. And I did not appreciate that my womenfolk had been at my diary. I suffered an overreaction. Such threats 'disturb me very much', I wrote, 'as I should not like to leave Granny'.

I had become a specialist in misfortune, repeating after Shelley: 'I fall upon the thorns of life! I bleed!' My 'distress' was carried forward from one journal entry to the next, and was not short of suitable settings in the lie of the land around me. Midlothian the beautiful was, at times, Midlothian the surly. There were places which gave off an intolerance of the human, which had the hardness of the pavement or playground against which a child might smack his whey face. Much of its beauty had survived from earlier times, from the 1790s, when the Whig lawyer and historian, Henry Cockburn, had roamed, as a boy, another High School boy, all the way to 'the deserts of Peebleshire': but much of the eyesore grimness that began to spread in the course of that century – when, during the hours of daylight, Gilmertonian women and boys toiled to the surface from the bowels of the earth, up ladders and along galleries, with their loads of coal – had also survived. A hundred and fifty years of industrial development had produced deserts very different from the ones roamed by Cockburn, and they have yet to bloom now that industries have taken their leave and the pits are shutting down. Jeanie Deans' wood, I notice, has become a rubbish dump.

At the village school, where teachers' reports had rated me 'dreamy', I had taken to dreaming my way past playground challenges, and to talking myself out of them. The fights and parliaments of the Gardens and of the school had coached me in a habit of defensive repartee, and a use of irony almost as enveloping as Sandy Brown's. Like Maggie Owen, I had been eager to learn new words, not all of them short. Knocked over in the playground, I had raised a smile by telling the teacher that I had 'collidded with another boy'. Words and books and girls were now swept up into a commitment to romance, to the legend which I sometimes thought my life had become, and which I was later to confide to the poetry pages of the school magazine in Edinburgh, *Schola Regia*. In those pages a poem by a friend was due to figure in which I was seen as a precarious angler, attacked by 'the crabs of unbelief' as I cast about in a pair of waders: 'Aloof contempt alone obscures your sense.' There was no mention of my brogues.

So far as my early diaries were concerned, I was not, in fact, an unbeliever. They indicate that I believed in a romantic God who was eventually to fill my shorts (which were about to become my longs), and my lumbar ganglia (when I started to read D. H. Lawrence), with passion. I once felt it on the surge as I stood at the sitting-room door, poised to cross over to the table on which my poems and my Classical vocabularies were laid out.

CHAPTER THREE

Rebecca's Vest

My earliest memory of a political response dates from the war: I was indignant when Attlee was rude to Churchill in the House of Commons. After that, for a while, I remember nothing political. My diary is virtually silent about the welfare state which was put in hand with the election of a Labour government in 1945. Nevertheless, it seems clear that a socialist outlook of a kind began when passion did. Adolescent selfishness, and its cult of misfortune, were at once to encourage and to constrain an interest in fellowship and fairness, in attacks on exploitation, in the flourishing of the muses to the benefit of the state, and in the more of these things that there had been during the war (together with the same old things, together with a ruling class). I was never for the enlargement of trade-union power which then came about, or for nationalising as much as possible. But I have aged into the condition of an unreconstructed believer in a welfare state and a health service, and in a national honour that requires them.

I was a Scottish patriot when I was young, but not a Scottish nationalist, and my sentiments have not changed. I should like to see a single country, Britain, which is several countries: to see regions, like the German *Länder*, to which a measure of real authority is assigned. The case for a separate Scotland is once more being urged, at a time when a Scottish culture appears to be thriving and many of the best Westminster politicians are Scots, when it is possible to read the novels of James Kelman, to watch 'Rab C. Nesbitt' on television, Govan's moving mad dog, and to listen to the Royal High's Labour politician Robin Cook. But it is also possible to do these things without feeling that they improve the case for separation. I have long thought of nationalism as in almost all respects an evil. Margaret Thatcher's nationalism, when the time came for that, and for its

29

inclusion among her miracles, did nothing to stop me – though it may well have made separatists of some wavering Scots.

At the age of fifteen, though, most of these thoughts lay in the future. At fifteen, I was Bloomsbury man in my preference for books and personal relationships. My diary made lists of the books I read, and I went on to award marks, out of a hundred. The first of these lists ran from November 1946 to July 1947: Scott's *Rob Roy, Charles II* by Arthur Bryant, J. W. Ferguson's play *Campbell of Kilmohr*, Lawrence's story 'Jimmy and the Desperate Woman', Robert Louis Stevenson's *Virginibus Puerisque*, Eric Linklater's autobiography *The Man on My Back,* Robert *Burns* by Hans Hecht, Linklater's book of dialogues *The Cornerstones*, Maupassant's 'Boule de suif', Balzac's *Eugénie Grandet*, Maurois's life of Shelley, *Ariel*, Liam O'Flaherty's autobiography *Shame the Devil*, Shaw's play *You Never Can Tell*, De Quincey's *Confessions of an English Opium Eater*, Scott's *Ivanhoe*, A. E. Housman's *The Name and Nature of Poetry*, a book of O'Flaherty's stories entitled *Civil War*, Joyce's *A Portrait of the Artist as a Young Man*, Aldous Huxley's novel *Time Must Have a Stop* and James Bridie's play *The King of Nowhere*.

Significant items on the next list included Herbert Read's *The Innocent Eye* (80 per cent), *Tess of the D'Urbervilles* (85), *Hamlet* (95), *The Turn of the Screw* (65), *Pride and Prejudice* (75), *Crime and Punishment* (85), Joyce's *Dubliners* (80), Stevenson's 'Thrawn Janet' (85), C. S. Lewis's *The Screwtape Letters* (75), Huxley's *Point Counter Point* (85), *Oedipus Rex* (91), Chekhov's 'My Life' (71), George Moore's *Confessions of a Young Man* (79) and Lawrence's confessions of another young man, *Sons and Lovers* (86), and Kant's *Lectures on Ethics* (ungraded).

Not much science here; a treatise on the physiology of sex hardly counts. And precious little philosophy. The lists show a taste for fiction, for the romantic, and for the confessions of young men. I took to Shakespeare and Donne, and I was fond of Scottish writers, Burns above all. And of foreign writers. Certain of the listed works were to leave a deep impression, imperfectly registered in the percentage points, where these were awarded. Among such works were Joyce's *Portrait*, Lawrence's

Sons and Lovers and the two novels by Aldous Huxley, whom I was presently to describe, for God's sake, as 'the God of literature'.

Carnal Miller – a mocking self-description – warmly sided with Huxley's Sebastian in *Time Must Have a Stop*, as he went about delivering himself of modern poems and satisfying his desires. The 'incandescent copulations of gods', 'twin cannibals in bedlam' – Huxley's brassy words for the sexual intercourse aspect of the sexual intercourse of things were music to my ears: I was indifferent to the way in which, as the novel reaches its stop, pictures of the 'cynical libertinage' of the modern world, in the ironic words of Sebastian's worldly uncle, give place to glimpses of an after-life. The novel is a late work by which few readers now can feel greatly affected, but it had its close reader in Gilmerton, Edinburgh, where it bore various unbeknown cues and precedents. It reeks of cigars. Sebastian's worldly uncle smokes them – they are his teat – and Sebastian smokes them too, and is made sick at his first attempt. The same thing happened to me, in London, and I have smoked them ever since.

Sebastian goes to Florence, with its mystic and its merry widow, and I was to go there a year or two later, at the same age of seventeen. My programme did not include any incandescent Mrs Thwale, but I did pay a visit to the villa of I Tatti, where I stood by Berenson's chaise-longue and eyed his fly-swatter, turning away to examine Proust's signature in a presentation copy of his great book (94?). In Florence itself there were, as for Sebastian, the titanesses of Michelangelo's Medici Chapel; and I witnessed the café where Auden wrote libretti and ate ice-cream (I had expected drugs), and where George Barker was to sit talking of the Cimabue Crucifixion in the entrance hall of the Uffizi Gallery, whose recesses he was, I was told, never to penetrate.

Sebastian, that 'small cherub in grey flannel trousers', was among the first of a succession of heroes with whom I found it hard to curtail my sympathy, obnoxious as they could occasionally be made to appear. This was one of the many books I was to read in which orphan attitudes – the genius as lost child, a lost child with most of the characteristics of the spoilt variety – exercised an urgent claim upon the reader. He reminded me, of course, of me, and of Verrocchio's fish-cuddling Florentine putto, who reminded me of round Dylan Thomas. I sent a postcard of the statue home to Edinburgh.

Another book which was to mean even more than I foresaw at the time when I read it was *Ivanhoe*. Handbooks to literature used to say that dark, injured and insulted Rebecca was 'more interesting' than beauteous, fair Rowena, and she was certainly very, very interesting to Walter Scott, who, while fully alive to her father's love for his shekels, dotes on Rebecca's outlandish looks and movie-star cleavage – which may well have paid tribute to his first encounters with the glamorous foreigner who became Lady Scott. Rebecca's

> form was exquisitely symmetrical . . . Her turban of yellow silk suited well with the darkness of her complexion. The brilliancy of her eyes, the superb arch of her eyebrows, her well-formed aquiline nose, her teeth as white as pearl, and the profusion of her sable tresses, which, each arranged in its own little spiral of twisted curls, fell down upon as much of a lovely neck and bosom as a simarre of the richest Persian silk, exhibiting flowers in their natural colours embossed upon a purple ground, permitted to be visible – all these constituted a combination of loveliness which yielded not to the most beautiful of the maidens who surrounded her. It is true that, of the golden and pearl-studded clasps which closed her vest from the throat to the waist, the three uppermost were left unfastened on account of the heat, which something enlarged the prospect to which we allude.

Rebecca and her vest, her loveliness, and, to be sure, the outrage suffered by this courageous victim, were very interesting to me too, as they have been to many readers over the years. They may be said to have helped to change our lives, and to have played a part in the Western philosemitism of the 1950s and 60s. 'Jewess' was to pass into my vocabulary as one of its most expressive items. Jews were few in Edinburgh, and these Jews had not been persecuted: they were also different, strange. Members of my family used to utter this synonym of mine for 'beautiful' as if it was a naughty or a risky word. As a reader of Scott, and of the tea leaves in my cup, I reckoned that Jeanie and the Jewess were sisters, but that Rebecca was more my kind of girl. Then again, such sisters might one day coincide.

I was only later to find out how deep has been the impression left by Isaac of York and his daughter, and to find out the tortuous extent of the fascination with Jews, both among their friends and among their enemies. Both parties have been compelled by this most compelling of foreign bodies. I learnt that anti-semitism had raved about the animal lasciviousness of the Jewess. Baudelaire had drawled about his *affreuse Juive* (when I first read about *her*, I did not presume anti-semitism – it was as who should say 'a frightful Norwegian'). This has imparted a tension to praise – among exogamous Gentiles, let us say – of a Jewish beauty. Mere reference to such a thing as Rebecca's vest has become well-nigh incorrect. In courting offence by referring to this garment, touching its hem, I am trying to speak the mind of my adolescence, and to summon up a state of affairs in which sympathy shared an environment and a conditioning with its opposite.

My diary entries for November 1946 have me, as so often, brooding over exams; a 'vague uneasiness' about results is spoken of as a good sign – but then I was by now rarely altogether easy about anything. I had taken to learning, or not learning, the fiddle, and to fouling the airs of a dance band that met for practice after school hours; I was to do the same for the school orchestra, as leader of the second violins. I told myself: 'You are interested in literature and the arts, and have consequently little time to play dance tunes. I honestly prefer the tunes of the masters.' A searing-swift notation then discloses that this owl had contracted the 'vice' of self-abuse – what else? The Greeks had a word for it, you might think from my diary, where 'masturbation' was transliterated – tucked away into what I took to be the safety of an ancient alphabet.

Soon afterwards I noted that the Russians had contracted the vice of allowing their 'Communistic ideals' to contaminate their art. I was reviewing the film *Ivan the Terrible*. 'I vaguely suspect them of distorting the facts in an attempt to make Ivan appear as one of the original Bolsheviks.' The theme was somewhat like that of *Lear*, but Ivan's arch-enemy was like the witch in *Snow White*. I loved the church music on the soundtrack – a far cry, or sublime sob, from the 'maddening drone' of the hymns in Liberton Kirk.

Prig, martyr, seeker of masters, Onan came second in those Form IVa exams. Another boy, as happens on such occasions, came first, and that boy was good both at lessons and at games. So committed to success was that boy's dad that he would take time off from his job to stand on the touchline at rugby games to check on his son's progress, and would put down pretenders, swots and sportsmen alike, with sweet smiles that must have helped to introduce them to the complexities of adult behaviour. This solicitude was the reverse of what I sometimes experienced, 'for my own good', at home, where progress wasn't much discussed and the young idea was scolded, and an aunt would tell me I 'looked terrible' – an Ivan.

When Christmas drew near, I moved to despising the seasonal intrusions of commerce and insincerity. There were too many presents and parties, and too few of them were for me. Christmas Eves were still spent scanning the sky for angels and for suitable weather – holy frost and snow to celebrate the arrival of the Christ Child. The winter of 1946 was depressingly clement. My youth was the last time when I was to feel a painful boredom, which would strike, as a rule, during the holidays. I would sit posted at the sitting-room window to inspect the nothing that was going on. One of my teachers, a vulnerable one, a modern poet who seemed as sad and thorn-prone as the most woebegone of my own outcast guises, came to my rescue at this point. I thought that he was like Baudelaire's albatross, whose giant wings trip him up when he goes about on land. He furthered my acquaintance with the obscurity, abstruseness and figurative density of 'rabid' Modernism. I was ripe for capture by the poetry of Dylan Thomas. But not without misgivings. 'Am I being too free? Is the *vers* too *libre*? I sincerely hope not.' That same Christmas I copied out pieces of Lawrence's story 'Jimmy and the Desperate Woman'. One of the pieces described a miner: 'His soul is a strange engine.' A strange engine myself, I took this in good part, as a reference to the men of Gilmerton and Newcraighall.

At the end of December I sent off a letter, a censure of P. G. Wodehouse, to the magazine *Illustrated*, which had offered to pay a guinea for such letters. I can't have suffered the necessary vague uneasiness about the outcome: no joy there. Joy had grown into a preoccupation of mine. The Presbyterian religion was against it. I was for it, and so was Robert Louis Stevenson, an Edinburgh man who had reached a conclusion about the Edinburgh virtues: 'If your morals make you miserable, depend upon it, they are wrong.' I was pleased that Stevenson should have chosen to speak of Robert Burns's 'panting after distinction' and 'desire to be in love'. Elsewhere, he speaks of his own 'feverish desire for consideration' when he was young – a romantic secularisation, this, of the Christian precept (set to music by Handel): 'Blessed be he that considereth the poor.'

Stevenson's statements seemed to fit my own strange case, and I also took to myself St Augustine's confession: *quaerebam quid amarem, amans amare.* I began to perceive that the desire for consideration may precede the desire for distinction, and that the desire to love can be hard to distinguish from the desire to be loved, which can be hard to distinguish from the ill-advised desire for fame.

On the last day of the year my thoughts were of Heaven. I was still looking forward to one, though it would not be like the 'perfectly organised receiving-station for the earthly bodies of the dead' which I'd come across in the film *A Matter of Life and Death*. Heaven had been remodelled in my mind to serve as a goal for the process of romantic self-creation. But what happened on the way was important too. Joy might happen. Once again, Stevenson's lessons applied: 'To travel hopefully is a better thing than to arrive.'

Girls and maths made my temples throb, my pulse quicken, my mouth a lime-kiln. Girls and maths were my Achilles heel, I told my diary. Not that Achilles can have kept a diary. Not that there were all that many girls about. Maths were about, though, with logarithms worse than algebra and far more obscure than modern poetry. On my first day back at school in the new year I was called to the blackboard to demonstrate a problem in trigonometry. I failed at that, and returned throbbing to my desk.

Embarrassment, exposure, was another of my heels. For someone who was willing to speak familiarly about fame, I was mostly shy when it came to showing myself in public. I wanted both to hide and to be seen, and in the clothes I went on to wear I observed a principle of retracted display, nervous effrontery, a principle honoured also in the keeping of a secret diary which some people might read – and in the publishing of a book which tells people what I don't want them to know. It was said that I could make fun but not take it. And it was also possible that I might indeed look terrible. Quite apart from anything else, there was the matter of my ears, which my father exhorted me to pin to my head by making sure that I slept on them at night, and there was the additional matter of the girlishness of this seeker of girls.

On the evening of the trigonometry ordeal I was to be seen at the Leith Links fair, in the company of a girl with the nice legs of the Forties and Fifties and with a head of absolutely black hair. She was of higher social standing, the daughter of a butcher thought to have done well out of the war, and she actually rode horses. This meant that I had a lot of conversation to produce as we rambled, the young, in one another's arms, round the fair. I entered a fortune-teller's tent. She was hung with shawls and petticoats – about her neck, an ivory horn. I crossed an elderly palm with silver and was told that I was to be very, very lucky and to have a great deal of money. I would go abroad. I would be 'led but not driven'. I would have six children and be 'a devil when I got to bed'. I felt I could forget my worries about sleeping on my ear. Who would have thought,

I wrote, that I would turn out to be 'a conjugal hedonist'. All this good news cheered me up after my humiliation. But it did not serve to bedevil my dealings with this new friend.

A vaporous Calvinist cold took charge of Edinburgh, and Calvinism was indicted in Carl Dreyer's film *Day of Wrath*, in which a granny was tortured by a witchfinder. 'I am a creature of the light,' I wrote in my book – the witchfinder's enemy. Much of that light came from my friendship with my own grandmother, who looked and dressed like the one in the film: she was 'the only person on this earth whom I love'. And yet my diary was filled with wails about needing someone to love. Half-way through February a skating holiday was declared at school: 'but of course I have done no skating.' I no more knew how to skate than I knew how to ride. But I had taken the ice by proxy long before I was born. There's a painting by Raeburn of a skater of the past – a stately leaning minister of the Kirk, large-hatted and all in black as he glides across Duddingston Loch with folded arms and lifted heel – and he has sometimes been thought to resemble me in appearance. I think of him as among my doubles, as the professional pupated from, yet simultaneous with, the tearful rebel.

A snowy Scotland rang with invectives aimed at Emanuel Shinwell's fuel cuts; I did not know who to blame in the matter. My next entry was written with an icicle. I resumed my pen to discuss attendance at Mrs Glendinning's Dancing Academy. 'Time has laid a heavy hand on the establishment,' and it had not neglected Ma Glendinning herself. I failed to master the steps and to make advances of the other kind – the wallflowers refused to flutter. I was also failing at the fiddle – taught me by the suave and patrician Waldo Channon, a humorous Englishman of parts, a tailored Englishman at that, all greys and roans, whose house in secluded, agreeable Anne Street, in the New Town, backed onto a brothel ruled by a rather more celebrated Ma. Mr Channon was obliged to administer a stylish reprimand. The world was not at my feet that bitter February. 'Many are cauld,' ran our schoolboy joke, 'but few are frozen.' My friends and I were frozen, and our religion was as ice.

37

In March the plot thinned. A neighbour reported us to the authorities for exceeding our allowance of coal. Not a likely story – we were not a family to take advantage, though I used to be sent out with a dustpan and brush to collect horse-droppings for the garden.

My Aunt Betty fell ill, and a diseased kidney had to be removed; later she was found to have tuberculosis, and went with a party of urban Scots to a Swiss sanatorium. Her falling ill was a shock. I had the grace to care about it, and to resolve to make myself 'as unobjectionable as possible' in the house. My own health was giving trouble, and I did justice to that too, confiding a plague of boils to my journal in a codicil to the Book of Job. A big one on the back of my neck had sent me stooping. Too much wartime concentrated orange juice, I diagnosed, at that early point in medical history, dosing myself with yeast. I was also plagued with eye trouble – too much reading of books, I feared – and a sort of 'mental vertigo'. My eyes were tested: I stared at the letters from between my sticking-out ears, and the right eye was pronounced weak. My mother had to pay the hair-raising sum of £2 12s. 6d. for a pair of reading specs, with delectable horn-rims. Despite these ailments, real and imaginary, my aunt's and my very own, I was able to brush up on my version of the felicific calculus by consulting the French Revolutionary aphorist, Chamfort – thought by Nietzsche to be the 'wittiest of all moralists': *Jouis, et fais jouir, sans faire de mal à personne – voilà toute la morale*. Had I known it at the time, I would have been rather less pleased by a further saying of Chamfort's. Ambition, he says, is 'serious imbecility', a grave infirmity of mind.

I went back to school after the Easter holidays to discover that there was a new English teacher. My commitment to the romantic, my wonderment at the modern, were to be sealed by what was to become a friendship. Hector MacIver had all of the charisma, and many of the shaping tutelary traits, of the novelist Muriel Spark's virtuoso schoolteacher Miss Jean Brodie, and he, too, was in his prime. He let us know that Yeats was the best poet there had been for a hundred and fifty years. I believed him – as I sat down out in Gilmerton to review that 'noble work' *Ivanhoe*, while noting that a certain Frenchman had said that Scott 'pauses at the threshold of the human soul'. So, I was later to decide, does Scott's biographer, John Buchan.

Hector had crossed that threshold, and several others. He was gifted and generous, handsome and courtly, with a touch of the features and bearing of Laurence Olivier. Born in the Hebrides, he had served as a Naval officer during the war. This soft-spoken foreigner had difficulty in reciting Burns, I noticed: this was not his language. Here was living proof of a truth which Scottish nationalism has yet to fathom: that Scotland has been two countries every bit as much as one. He was a Gael and a storyteller in the Celtic mode, a writer, a director of plays, a lover of books and of whisky. He lodged near the school in the house of the old scholar Herbert Grierson, where Yeats had been a caller, and he would hold court in Grierson's Donne-haunted library, glanced into by its garden trees, when he wasn't in one of his pubs. He was a friend of Hugh MacDiarmid and of Louis MacNeice, and he was to become a friend of Dylan Thomas. He lifted me towards a heady world where writers might step from their books into your company. His influence is rapidly apparent in my journal: in its attention, for instance, to A. E. Housman's claim that 'to transfuse emotion – not to transmit thought' was the purpose of poetry. I had yet to be confronted with Eliot's more debatable claim that poetry was 'an escape from emotion'. One way and another, Hector's arrival was very emotional.

That summer he produced, at the school, a Second World War play by Jack Alldridge, *All This is Ended*, in which I played the part of a soldier with an illegitimate child, who had to agonise over 'Lilly and the kid' – to the derision of the kids in the playground and the scandal of my aunts, who felt that the play was pure pornography. It closed amid plaudits and some 'constructive and intelligent criticism in the *Scotsman*'. Having been defeated by my part, and by the art of acting on the stage, I persuaded myself that 'the play was poorly written.'

At Hector's suggestion, I read Herbert Read's memoir *The Innocent Eye*, a favourite book among the adults I knew. I felt that it was good to be sensitive, and to be so, like the young Read, in the country; I was a country boy myself, with an innocent eye as well as a weak one. I proceeded to Hardy's *Tess*, admiring it for its Lilly and the kid, despite its 'incorrigible fatalism', and despite having turned against Victorian fiction (most of it by Dickens) after an immersion between the ages of nine and twelve. The school year came to an end with a debate in which I argued that no one should be forced to go to school beyond the age of twelve, or to take part in sport. I was scorned, to a storm of applause, for playing no games myself and lacking team spirit. I didn't think to reply that I did play a game, the national game, officially disdained at the Royal High. We then put on our whites for the annual prize-giving and for the annual concert at the Usher Hall.

During the first week of July I paid visits to the sick – to Betty in her nuns' nursing home, and to Hector, who had gone down with dysentery when *All This* had ended, and was dosing himself with laudanum in old-fashioned romantic style. I went with him to see *Lady Windermere's Fan*, and dashed off my review. I went to Liberton Kirk and reviewed the sermon, after which he and I inspected a Catholic church where the priest of some years before had been one of the originals of Wilde's delinquent, duplex Dorian Gray: this was John Gray, who was to dawn on me, many years later, as a preposterous Nineties poet who had a talent for writing poetry. Hector and I were on the flirt with a swooning Fin-de-Siècle Catholicism – not to be confused with the dismal-hysterical Irish variety from which James Joyce had plotted his escape.

John Gray's poems are period pieces which can be seen to have moved with the medium to new ground, towards the poetry of Modernism. They have the leaps and bounds of the flying fish which meets its fate in one of the best of them: the ballad of a metaphysical pirate which Dylan Thomas would or must have liked, and which I would have liked to have known when I first read Dylan Thomas. Elsewhere, Gray confesses:

> I dreamed I was a barber; and there went
> Beneath my hand, oh! manes extravagant.

Such extravagance, however, was renounced. The 'sins' and exotic pleasures of the period, and the profile and pastel looks and bee-stung lips of its young male beauties, were put behind him, and he became a priest.

> There liveth no Tobias graced with power
> To take angelic counsel, to uproot
> Swarth lust, meek purity to substitute,
> But meets the angel in the proper hour.

Having met the angel, shed his delinquent double, he went off *in partibus infidelium* – from London to Edinburgh, where, less fleetingly than I was about to do, he served the poor in the lower depths of the Cowgate. Then, in the city's refined Morningside district, where manes are seldom extravagant, the Italianate church of St Peter's was built to his taste by Lorimer. In the priest's house he slept the sleep of the saved, between black linen sheets – but with a bag of golf clubs in the hall. Two lines from his conversion turmoil are very appealing:

> Ignorant, besotted,
> Even in despair effete.

In me too, 'swarth lust' had taken root. Having recognised 'a certain affinity' between my state of mind and that of Huxley's Sebastian ('the same poetic sensibility and the same obsessing, irresistible sensuality'), I switched to a kinship with the young man of Joyce's *Portrait*. I copied out a passage in which Stephen is shamed by his desires: 'The letters cut in the stained wood of the desk stared upon him, mocking his bodily weakness and futile enthusiasms and making him loathe himself for his own mad and filthy orgies.' My body too, I reckoned, was weak. It was 'like a door which has not been opened for many years; it is rusty, difficult to open and overgrown with weeds.' The 'wasting fires of lust' (Joyce) had been at it: but it could still manage to insert a semi-colon, and it was to write an especially poor poem entitled 'The Wasting Fires'.

I read on in Joyce's beckoning book. 'He moaned to himself like some baffled prowling beast ... He wanted to sin with another of his kind, to force another being to sin with him and to exult with her in sin.' There was too much guilt here for someone who had lost more of his former outlook than Stephen had, but I knew what he meant. 'I can't understand myself,' I wrote. But I understood that I was tongued by wasting fires, and I began to tell myself that I had to be the air-raid warden who extinguished them, or, less mundanely, and in the rhetoric of adolescence, that I had to practise the magic art of the phoenix and rise Lawrentian from their ashes.

Others of my age were to read these books and to experience what I am recalling, and to inquire, as I did, into the history of our situation. It seemed that a declared opposition to the sermon which said that sexual activity was wrong, to the priestly function of binding with briars our joys and desires, had come and gone for two centuries and more. A recent push had been administered by those hostile to the proprieties associated, somewhat indiscriminately, with the Victorians, and further pressure had resulted from changes of mind occasioned by the two world wars. It was as if we had mostly gone up and up of late, and were now trembling on a cusp. There was tension, crisis, in the Thirties bungalow and the Forties air-raid shelter, and the interest in sex would sometimes wax anxious and extreme. Tyrannic love, panged with uncertainty. Even those who thought highly of love could continue, as earlier in the century, to think of the bodily business as dirty and devilish (the sex lives of Yeats and Shaw testify to an Irish pre-eminence in this area).

In the course of the Sixties a new freedom is generally felt to have been achieved, one which the middle-aged may have been inclined to attribute to their struggles, for struggles they were in their way. It gave more to men than it did to women, however, and there were many to whom it gave nothing more than a sense of the misery and disorder that ensue on the collapse of empires. Exodus from the closet continues, while the brutal and licentious have remained brutal and licentious, and continue to make what they can of the new situation. But it is a situation which is unlikely to last much longer. Old fears have returned with the outbreak of Aids, and will no doubt do their bit to bring back programmes of repression.

The other night I had a dark mezzotint dream, of a festive London, with crowds parading down Whitehall, as crowds did in protest at the time of the Suez war, and with scuffles breaking out. This was a day of licence, on which it would be all right for people to get off with each other. My friend Ian Hamilton appeared to me to say, in his terse fashion, that he'd had twenty approaches. I told him that I'd had none, and that this was because I'd gone to the festival with my mother – though the dream had shown me that I'd gone with my daughter.

'Dreams are aye contrar,' my grandmother used to remark, and I take this, so far as it is true, to bear witness to the further truth that nearly everything has two meanings or more. In this particular dream, at all events, contrary senses can be made out, and there was indeed something funny about the passage of history at which the dream seems to direct its incestuous murmur. The ambiguity of liberation, of the sexual intercourse which began, according to Philip Larkin, and without poor Philip Larkin, in 1963, can be noticed in the dream, and so can a preoccupation which began to enter the nights of my middle age, and which was to issue in an equivocal little poem, where my mother is flat out in bed and I have to break the door down to get into the room.

> I thought I saw my mother. There were snaps
> Of someone else's children in her hand.

CHAPTER FOUR

Rampion

'*'T*is the bright day that brings forth the udder.' Another
schoolboy joke, this, exchanged with a friend in the
doorway of a sweetshop in Waterloo Place. The sun had come
to Scotland at last. Towards us stepped astounding girls in thin
dresses, with displays of cleavage to gladden the heart of Walter
Scott, whose Gothic monument shot up black, beyond the black
bulk of the North British Hotel and the nether world of Waverley Station, into a shimmering blue sky.

There I was on my holidays in the summer of 1947, a pain in
the neck, a boil about to burst. Master Thorn, Master Bates.
The sunlight soon faded from the pages of my diary, and in the
autumn I wrote: 'My forehead is flushed and lined, my nose is
red and marked with spots, while my hair is dirty, colourless
and lifeless. O unlovable!' I could always have washed my hair.
It was as if I needed these defects – as stigmata, outward and
visible signs of the isolation and misfortune of which the diary
continued to complain. And yet around me were friendly faces
and companion spirits, relatives who looked after me, teachers
who encouraged me. With the assistance of the books I was
reading and of the one I was writing, I was in some danger of
turning into a fraud.

As far as life-chances were concerned, I couldn't have complained that I was worse-off than my Aunt Kate and my Uncle
Tom, the family's simple souls. They did not get on, and used to
scare me when I was small by scrapping over possession of the
Edinburgh Evening News. About scraps I had long been seriously
torn, as an early short story, written for my mother about a
quarrel at the Kirkcaldy Links fairground, seems to indicate: 'I
saw two men fighting one of the men socked a punsh on the
other mans jaw and skined his cheek then the man that had hurt
the other man said to the man come here and I will smash you

and so the other man didnt go.' I was both of these men, the one who said come here and the one who didn't go. My drawings of the same date were all of socking punches and banging guns, of sepoys downing tribesmen in the last throes of the Raj. I liked football, and football, whatever else it was, was a fight. I wanted to beat the village toughs but couldn't, and had to learn to talk them out of it, having learnt to dislike it, just as I had to learn to talk girls into it, such as it then was, that other 'it'. The two 'it's' were, in fact, sometimes to seem identical. I was breathing the air of a society which had long believed what Lawrence was to tell it – that 'the act of love is a fight'; a society for whose males the thought of the lion that tumbles the deer and eats it up, tender neck and sad eye rearing from its passionate attentions, was erotic.

In the August of this year there was a household drama which starred Kate and Tom, whose simplicity could be felt to threaten embarrassment on the rare occasions when the family went public. Kate worked in the town but often came to stay. I remember her tears, the blush of grief on her face, her surgical boots, the Veet for removing superfluous hair. I see her standing at the back door with a lump of coal in her hand, having called as an inadvertent 'first foot' one New Year's morning, when it was bad luck for first feet, her own poor feet included, to arrive empty-handed, and been adjured from the kitchen window to go round to the back and collect the token gift. On this occasion a party from the South was expected – my Uncle Bob, his wife and her father, an amiable old-world Lancashire businessman. We were nerved to be on our best behaviour, to keep our elbows off the table and avoid showing ourselves up, and Kate and Tom were to be kept from the limelight. I gave the sardonic laugh that echoes in my diary at this time. Kate gasped that 'we didn't want them to see her,' and took up her coat to go back to the maternity home at which she helped with the babies and washed their nappies. Eventually she was slipped into the sitting-room, where the guests were seated: 'Thus did Cinderella arrive at the ball.' Tom had retired, virtuously, to the back bedroom.

After the ball was over, the guests left for their hotel in Edinburgh – the same hotel where Bob and Ida had stayed during the war and which had generated a curious tale of love locked out. One evening in the dining-room they'd been struck by the conversation of a sympathetic and well-educated couple, a girl soldier in the ATS and a Polish officer, and then in the dead of night a thunderous knocking had broken out. The manager had proceeded to expel the couple from the hotel for being in the same bed. People might seem nice, but look what they could get up to, ran the thought. It was all right for these two to be killed in the war, all wrong for them to sleep together. Romantic values, and the tide of objection to thoughts of this kind, caused me, in silence, to bless the bed on which they had lain. There were no such beds, I reflected, at No 54 Moredun Park Gardens, which I needed to consider a preserve of vestals and severity. In time to come, I was to say to my bride as I led her across the threshold: 'No one has ever had sexual intercourse in this house.'

August and September showered me with books, plays, films, friends and excursions. I don't believe that I can ever have imagined that I was living in a backwater, and I wasn't. I believed that my friends were gifted and interesting, and so they were. One of my geniuses lived just up the road from me and attended the same school – Alec Kelly, a pianist. I went with him for blethering walks. In Rosslyn Chapel, an ancient place I've resorted to ever since, we gazed at the Prentice Pillar, carved by another genius in the absence of his master, who had gone to Rome to obtain a design for the pillar and the consent of the Pope. The master returned to find that the pillar had been swathed in vine tendrils which descended to a base where serpents were devouring the fruit: in a rage, he struck the pupil dead. I blessed the pupil, and ranked him with the lovers in the hotel.

The recently devised and not exactly indigenous Edinburgh Festival had started its season, and I was due to be a stage page – to carry a torch in the Glyndebourne production of Verdi's *Macbeth*. I watched a Ballets Jooss performance of their antiwarmonger work *The Green Table* – a masterpiece, I gathered, of Modern Dance. It seemed that Modern Dance, or Free Dance, as it was also called, was engaged in seeing off Classical Ballet; it had become possible to reflect that Sybil Thorndike and Pavlova – two of Miss Jean Brodie's cherished artists in the Edinburgh of a decade before which is evoked in Muriel Spark's novel – had been deposed by Arletty and Martha Graham.

I had written to my mother at the age of five, 'Will u sed me a bok for I wont wun,' and I was more of that mind than ever. It was at this point that I read *Pride and Prejudice* and *The Turn of the Screw*. I disliked what I took to be the snobbery of the first and the laboured syntax of the second, acknowledging the horror of the 'infamous' valet while accepting – what I was later to question – the authority of the governess's narrative. *Crime and Punishment* was something else. I loved it. And I loved the film *Les Enfants du Paradis*, with sloe-eyed Arletty and Alec Kelly-like Jean-Louis Barrault. Alec Guinness's Richard II didn't always reach me in the gods, where I always sat. Then Hector MacIver got back from the Hebrides and we listened to an evening of Gaelic songs – sounds from another world. My cup was full.

It ran over when, at the King's Theatre where I was paging, I made friends with a dancer who was performing in the entr'actes of the operas. This was his chore. He was really a choreographer and a Modern Dancer. Ernest Berk had been brought up in Germany and he and his wife Lotte had come to this country as refugees. Half-English, he displayed a German earnestness and intensity. *Ernst ist das Leben, heiter ist die Kunst* – he said to me what Schiller had said to him, and his very name and nature were lodged in the precept. Life was serious and art joyful, and Modern Art was especially joyful. So Modern was he that everything that had happened yesterday or the day before could be made to seem a little displeasing – even Beethoven, whose symphonies he blamed for measuring out their profundities in the manner of a man descending band by band within some barrel. Art was joyful, and you should just plunge down into the barrel, not thinking to scrape it or sound it.

One Sabbath we decided to take a walk and I picked him up at his digs, where I found him with Lotte – a dancer too, sable-tressed, wax-white skin, dressed in pyjamas and dressing-gown, warm and funny. Rebecca and her vest had come to life. No walker, though. Her afternoons were spent listening to her friends in the Vienna Philharmonic Orchestra rehearsing Mahler's *Das Lied von der Erde*. Ernest and I set off from Leith Walk up the Calton Hill, overlooking my school, down into the Canongate, up the Royal Mile to the Tron Kirk, along Rankeillor Street into the King's Park, past the palace of Holyrood, up round the Salisbury Crags and then up to the summit of Arthur's Seat.

Like other older friends of mine, he gave the impression of an unforced interest in what I had to say – more of a gift than I realised at the time. He explained that he had completed a ballet called *Dionysus 47* (after the year) – with jazz music and Bacchanals and a thesis about the balance between the physical and the spiritual. The physical had begun to pour with rain as we scaled Arthur's Seat, rags of mist floating up from the valley beneath. We got to the top, to the brow of the very hill – 'the pinnacle of the rocky precipice' – where, in James Hogg's *Confessions*, innocent George Wringhim is approached by his brother Robert, whose 'dark eyes gleam on him through the mist', their intensity 'hardly brookable'. Ernest's intensity was exhilarating. His eyes were none the worse for gleaming with a not altogether humorous joyfulness as he spoke about sex. Pure but sexual, Ernest was to distrust Hector's eyes when he studied their ironic, uningenuous gaze in a photograph of the cast of our recent play. Ernest was, in a sense, like Robert Wringhim's tempter and demon, Gilmartin, who tells him the very thing he is alert and has been schooled to hear. He tells him that the saved can do no wrong. And indeed this may have been construed by me as an aspect of Ernest's gospel too.

He asked me if I had a girlfriend. 'Yes,' I replied, the right answer being no. Had I ever had sexual relations with a girl? Words failed me as the rain came down; I wasn't up to the reply that I had a girlfriend with whom I hadn't had sexual relations.

In Germany, it appeared, before Nazism, relations between the sexes had been natural and free. 'The emotional life of each individual,' ran my journal paraphrase of what I heard on the hill, 'is centred on sex, which is the most potent and important force in life.' I agreed with Ernest about that. Pre-marital intercourse was 'not a thing to be sedulously avoided'. Unacted desires were bad for me. He also said that my aim should not be 'to make a name for myself', but to try to 'formulate a life-philosophy which would be worthwhile', and I accepted the rebuke.

The sexual intercourse aspect of James Hogg's sexual intercourse of things had been eloquently expounded, to a willing ear, on James Hogg's Arthur's Seat. Robert Wringhim's first meeting with Gilmartin takes place on 25 March 1704, when he has 'just entered the eighteenth year of my age'. My conversation with Ernest took place on 7 September 1947, when I had just turned sixteen. It could be thought that Robert and I had each been his own tempter.

I went brimming back to school for my second-last year, newly demonic and Blakean, with the wish to be as frank and free and pure and nude as any *Wandervogel*, and with my appetite for the modern refreshed. This did not exempt me from a dull person's witnessing of *Murder in the Cathedral* ('complex'), from perhaps preferring the Thackeray of *Henry Esmond* to Dickens, or from attending evening service with Hector at the Episcopalian Cathedral of St Mary's. I read Synge's play *Deirdre of the Sorrows* ('It is not I will be back soon in Emain' – I couldn't be doing with that sort of thing). I experienced a more congenial Celtic twilight in Hector's talk on Second Sight to the school Literary Society. And I gave up the fiddle.

In November I met 'Sheena', a 'very nice' girl with black hair and a white face a little like Shelley's, attractive and intelligent, with half an ear at most for the discourse of freedom and nudity. Nevertheless, 'we were to shock everyone around us at the New Victoria Cinema with the tenderness of our love-making.' The journal is referring to a small quantity of 'quiet, unimpassioned sensuality'. A week later, however, I was informed by my grandmother that we had been spied on by a 'disgusted' someone from Liberton. 'Knowing our circumstances,' said she, Miss or Mrs Someone had written a letter to 'apprise my family', as the journal put it, 'of my split personality'. Knowing our circumstances my granny! It did not occur to me that my womenfolk had been reading the journal of my secret life and that there was no such spy.

When I came to write a book on doubles, split personality, literary duality, I had forgotten that one of its themes had been concisely stated in my diary by way of response to this alleged surveillance: 'They treat me like an outcast. I shall break out soon.' The book was to see itself as studying a literature whose authors and heroes want both to break in and to break out, are at once imprisoned and excluded, mild and wild, good and bad. I had served as my own example.

Sheena gave as good as she got in her dealings with the chatterbox confessional amorists by whom she was desired and respected. My friendship with her lasted on and off till the following summer, when I spent an evening on her sofa moving my hand ever so slightly and slowly up her leg until at a certain critical point her own escorting hand became a vice, while the school choir, from which I had defected, boomed brown from the wireless-set with Longfellow's Hiawatha trochees and other pieces of oratorio and elocution: purity and nudity and freedom were to suffer a defeat. Sheena's leg led up to the highest peak in the Southern Uplands. It was harder to ascend than Arthur's Seat, or than F6 – Auden's magic mountain, which, along with Thomas Mann's, I was presently to attempt from my armchair at No 54. Before long, she married a large boy who was often silent.

I was a boy for whom it was a marvel that a French lector at school should turn out to be a 'good friend' of Jean-Louis Barrault, my *enfant du paradis*. Such marvels were now quite frequent. It was as if I couldn't make a friend who wasn't a good friend of Shelley or Stravinsky. I had already seen Shelley plain in the persons of the writers who had enacted the 'Scottish Renaissance' in Edinburgh's Mermaid taverns. The pre-eminent

Hugh MacDiarmid would come in from his cottage in the country, beyond the Pentlands.

His authority rested on his lyrics of the Twenties, done in the artificial-polemical 'synthetic' Scots that became known as Lallans. He told me later in London, in a taxi by the Thames, one of the things he liked to say on the subject: that his strange words from dictionaries and from the distant past had been put in to 'aggrandise' the verse. The word, with the stress on the last syllable, rose up in the cab like some rock or landmark – it was as if he'd said 'Ravenscraig' or 'Corrievreckan'. His strange words inhabit lines of poetry which were immediately apparent, when Hector showed them to me, as Scottish speech, and which are, indeed, otherwise unutterable. To borrow a term from a metrical formula of Robert Frost's, they are imparted to a 'sound of sense', and that sound, and sense, are Scottish.

Several poems from the magnificent harvest of the Twenties feel for the predicament of some wee lassie, and one of them – which tells of a girl singing to a child that is no longer there – sounds the native note, to perfection, in the second of its two stanzas. None of the words here are strange, except to English ears. But this is the note on which, elsewhere, to revert to the Frost formula, his strange words are 'strung' – gathered from books and strung together with words 'gathered by the ear from the vernacular'.

> Wunds wi warlds to swing
> Dinna sing sae sweet,
> The licht that bends owre a'thing
> Is less ta'en up wi't.

Here is a compassion which is Scottish, but of which Scotland has always stood badly in need.

The strange words of this aggrandisement were put in to establish a severance from sentimental Scotticism, from the Kailyaird. They seem to me to have very little to do with any generic heightening of the kind associated with the poetic diction of the Augustan eighteenth century. But neither do they un-equivocally represent an avant-garde refusal of the demotic, drawn though MacDiarmid presently was to avant-garde attitudes.

MacDiarmid is famously equivocal, and this diction is both native and strange. He was also drawn both to Communism and Fascism. The paradox of his mingling of the two rhetorics, in the commandments issued in his polemical prose writings, had long been in place when I came to know him, and his poetry had moved from Lallans to a discursive English stalled (for me) in a different order of aggrandisement. In the early poems he was a romantic Moon man, like William Drummond of Hawthornden: many of them swing with galactic winds and look down on the Earth in the manner of an Apollo astronaut. Like Drummond, too, he was to be thought a plagiarist, for his occasional liftings and transcriptions. These were the accident and design of a driven lifetime; they belong both to the copious contents, the welter, of his country cottages and to the repetitions and re-doings that are inherent in more than one species of poetry. The charge is never likely to detract from the recognition due to an adventurous achievement. He is one of the more abrasive heroes, and his trip was always to run the risk of burning up. But for Scottish poetry he was a life after death. 'A new deil is aye lichtsome,' as a proverb of the country declares, a proverb which has appealed to his friend, the poet Norman MacCaig. MacDiarmid was a new devil who was lightsome and awesome, and at times a terror, seeking whom he might devour. For my part, I have to say that I was never as much as bitten.

I think of him in his armchair, at his cottage in the corner of a field near Biggar, surrounded by his mementoes like some old guerrilla general; of that head of hair, twisting up whelk-like from the thinker's brow and darkly-circled anxious eyes, the clustered features of a small face; of the black bar of bitter pipe tobacco, which you had to carve with a knife. In a poem for the centenary of his birth in 1892, Seamus Heaney writes of his Shetland days, of

> Your big pale forehead in the window glass
> Like the earth's curve on the sea's curve to the north.

He is seen here, in one of his aspects, as 'thrawn', and he is also seen as

having us on,
Setting us off, the drinker's drinker . . .

I remember his doctor speaking of the 'constitution' which had enabled him to survive all this amber and bitter black, to survive his crises and the efforts of his genius. There were to be over eighty years of this duet of the anxious and the robust.

Side by side with his friend, Norman MacCaig was the image of nonchalance, *le poète allongé*, who may also, however, have been mistaken by some, in a bad light, for MacDiarmid's minder, looking after him on his visits to the wicked city. For me, he was a writer of equal virtue, and a man whose charm might have melted the Scott Monument and split the Calton Hill. From the early days of my visits to his flat near the King's Theatre, in one of Edinburgh's roomy, firesided slate-grey tenements – where I would read his typescripts, poems that were then on the turn from the surrealism of the Apocalyptic school to modes you could call, for short, and invidiously, Movement-compatible – to the day when I left the city, he was a sustaining friend. With half his heart in the Highlands, he had set himself to write, in English, poems that would be his 'medicine', as landscape was to be his 'religion'. He was a schoolteacher in those days, and he had been to the school that I was attending, as had Andrew Young, who also wrote his poetry in English, and who moved away to join the Scots diaspora. They are exponents of the same version of pastoral. Meanwhile another High School alumnus, Robert Garioch, chose to write for the most part in a satirical town Scots, whose elegant growls pay tribute to Robert Fergusson's versifying of eighteenth-century Edinburgh and to the epistolary Burns. Scotland's warring categories – town and country, Highland and Lowland, Scots words and English words, God and no God – are commemorated in the choices made by these three former pupils of the same school.

Both Young and MacCaig were to revere the mountain Suilven in the North-West of Scotland, and to make it seem as beautiful as its name. A canon of his Church, like John Gray, Young was to think of Suilven in his English cathedral.

The mountain in my mind burns on,
As though I were the foul toad, said
To bear a precious jewel in his head.

Accounted Georgian in the Fifties, having fallen down the cracks between Scotland and England, ancient and modern, he seems to have been left to lie there.

This was the time when I decided that Aldous Huxley was a god. In the autumn of that year, 1947, I read *Point Counter Point*, written twenty years earlier. It was like one of my new friends, in that it gave access of a sort to writers and other notables – Lawrence, Middleton Murry, Augustus John, Oswald Mosley – while telling me what I had begun to think. When I read it again recently, I found in it a contribution to the perennial literature of duality. I did not hear the voice of any god.

The novel describes, among much else that is uninviting, a brutish and inarticulate working class, by which I did not imagine, when I was young, that he might have meant me. I did not dream that good writers could be snobs. Nor did I dream – though this is hardly Huxley's case – that literature incorporates a snobbery which suggests disturbance of mind. I did not know what, in 1922, Virginia Woolf had had to say in her journal about the working-class egotist who had written *Ulysses*: '. . . a queasy undergraduate scratching his pimples . . . An illiterate, underbred book it seems to me; the book of a self taught working man, and we all know how distressing they are, how egotistic, insistent, raw, striking, and ultimately nauseating.' Had I come across the passage, with its 'we' who 'all know', I might have thought it a mad description of Joyce. As a description of the author of my own journal, it has, I suppose, its telling points.

Huxley's novel is never as distressed, and distressing, as Woolf's *Writer's Diary*, in its attentions to the working class and to the egotistical writers of that class. It may be said, after all, to propound, in its sarcastic way, the doctrines of one of the insistent underbred. It speaks of the restoration of a balance, of the whole man, of a human truth which may heal the division between body and soul, instinct and intellect. Who and where are these whole men? 'One might still find a few of them in Italy.' And it would appear that there are one or two of them about in England. And there were lots of them in the remote past, in the days before division. England's whole man might suggest a modern Man of Feeling – the aroused sensorium of the romantic past. He is a special person. While intent on a simple life, he is pretty sure to be waited on by a servant or two. He is not a member of the abject and inchoate masses. Wholeness is scarce, in a world poisoned by intellectualism and Don Juanism.

The novelist Philip Quarles, a self-critical portrait of the artist, is receptive to the views expressed by the D. H. Lawrence character, Mark Rampion, and a sufferer from the disease that Rampion is out to cure. Intensely conscious, he is 'tired of consciousness', indifferent to other people, including his wife, estranged from the masses. In this last respect, we may be meant to sympathise with him: he is against jazz and 'listening-in' to the radio, and so was Huxley, whose preface to his anthology *Texts and Pretexts* sneers at 'what the negroes bawl through the noise of the saxophones'. He lights on 'a new way of looking at things' in fiction, which is apparent in the novel we are reading. The new way is simultaneous multiplicity – looking at things with many eyes at once: 'With religious eyes, scientific eyes, economic eyes, *homme moyen sensuel* eyes . . .' Plot doesn't matter in the new novel, 'because everything's implicit in anything. The whole book could be written about a walk from Piccadilly Circus to Charing Cross.' Huxley's novel cleaves to that terrain, with excursions north to Soho and Bloomsbury, west to Belgravia, and east to Juhu Beach in Bombay. Perhaps this is the whole book that a whole man might be empowered to write.

Rampion, the self-styled atavismus, delivers a big speech which I copied out with care. 'At the basis of my philosophy will be the ideas propagated by Rampion.' Not that I was to be without misgivings in the months that followed. I smelt something of 'the thriller or the pornographic paperback' in Huxley's novels. 'I come to extravagant conclusions about him.' But I was all for this speech of Rampion's:

'Blake was civilised,' he insisted, '*civilised*. Civilisation is harmony and completeness. Reason, feeling, instinct, the life of the body – Blake managed to include and harmonise everything. Barbarism is being lopsided. You can be a barbarian of the intellect as well as of the body. A barbarian of the soul and the feelings as well as of sensuality. Christianity made us barbarians of the soul, and now science is making us barbarians of the intellect. Blake was the last civilised man.'

The views expressed in the novel go back to the ancient world, but there is more to this than the impression that Rampion is the sort of revolutionary who wants to see a return to some golden age. He is more of a traditionalist than his author seems to realise. Again and again he teaches the lesson that 'you try to be more than human, but you only succeed in making yourself less than human.' No one could successfully have claimed in 1928 that this belonged to a new way of thinking. In the 1830s the adage was cited, in a fit of caution or contrition, by flighty Edgar Allan Poe: 'In efforts to soar above our nature, we invariably fall below it.' At this point in the novel Baudelaire's clumsy albatross is introduced, as a kind of anti-phoenix, in order to insist that we should beware of wings.

Seven years before Huxley's book was published, Eliot was saying that Donne was the last civilised man, and contributing to the literature of duality by inventing the doctrine of a dissociation of sensibility from thought, first manifested in seventeenth-century England. The doctrine is shaken by the epigraph to *Point Counter Point*: a passage of verse by a contemporary of Donne's, Fulke Greville, whose chorus of priests, in a play of his, speaks of the 'wearisome condition of humanity' and affirms that 'passion and reason self-division cause.' Eliot explained that we had 'never recovered' from the dissociation of sensibility which set in after Donne. Tennyson and Browning 'do not feel their thought as immediately as the odour of a rose. A thought to Donne was an experience; it modified his sensibility.' Meanwhile Greville writes as if self-division has had a long history, and a connection with the fall of man. Men are 'created sick, commanded to be sound'. The old Adam was two old Adams. Eliot's doctrine was of its time, which was one of the many times, some of them very distant, when dualistic explanations were more than usually appealing to literary people.

Huxley's novel refers to the literature of duality. He mocks his lecherous editor Burlap (a slur on the well-winged Middleton Murry) by having him exchange letters with a poetess who turns up at the office to reveal herself as a lesbian duo known to itself as Jekyll and Hyde. At another point he could be taken to allude to a passage in the poetry of Donne, and thereby to Eliot's intervention in the history of duality. 'Her pure and eloquent blood,' wrote Donne of Elizabeth Drury,

> Spoke in her cheeks, and so distinctly wrought,
> That one might almost say, her body thought.

Huxley writes here of a radical wholeness: 'Her lips responded hardly less closely and constantly to her thoughts and feelings than did her eyes, and were grave or firm, smiled or were melancholy through an almost infinitesimally chromatic scale of emotional expression.'

It is an upper-class woman's body which is doing the thinking – that of Mrs Quarles, Philip's mother. A few pages later we are told in Darwinian vein that 'human beings have only a limited number of noises and grimaces with which to express the multiplicity of their emotions.' It is a 'cockney' woman who has caused Huxley to contradict himself – and who has been made a monkey of. This is Mrs Quarles's husband's fancy woman, Gladys. Gladys's body doesn't think, and she herself is given little to do save scheme and be vulgar and say 'Ta'. Her sexual encounters with her buffoon lover come in for heavy disparagement. This Huxley is a fan of the instinctual who is apt to be disparaging when his characters set themselves to make love: it's as if he'd like to drop a dog on them from a passing aeroplane, as in *Eyeless in Gaza*. He is also responsible, in the earlier novel, for one of the most unpleasant scenes in the literature of the time: the self-consciously indifferent account of the death of Philip's child from meningitis.

Seen in the book as a puritan, Rampion is the sort of puritan who calls for a 'genuine phallism. And if you imagine it has anything to do with the unimpassioned civilised promiscuity of our advanced young people, you're very much mistaken indeed.' He believes that civilised is uncivilised in this day and age, that advanced is backward, that nearly everyone since Blake has been very much mistaken indeed, and that Shelley was a 'fairy slug with the sexual appetites of a schoolboy'. The schoolboy who read this twenty years after it was published may have felt that it was unfair both to schoolboys and to Shelley and his thorns: but he had made up his mind that his appetites had better be impassioned, rather than, as in the New Victoria Cinema, 'unimpassioned'.

For all the glibness and occasional grimness of the rhetoric it contains, the book has a case to present which can, I think, in certain of its elements, still be respected, and which may well, for a while, have been almost as influential as any of Lawrence's own versions of the doctrine. It is not difficult to be moved, for instance, by Rampion's enthusiasm for the words of the Anglican marriage service: 'With my body I thee worship.' That autumn, Prince Philip was worshipping Princess Elizabeth with his body, and their marriage service employed these words, which the Church of England has since stupidly deleted. I liked the thought of his thinking body performing this worship. But I was haughty about his styling himself the Duke of Edinburgh. Their marriage was celebrated with a holiday from school and with a fireworks portrait of the pair in the night sky.

Point Counter Point is a satire which is also a tract. It can seem to descend from Wilde's *Dorian Gray*, and from Saki's *The Unbearable Bassington* of 1912. The three works share the preoccupation with duality, and with advanced talk in expensive places, that ran from the 1880s on. 'I think I must have a sort of double brain,' remarks one of Saki's ladies, and Lady Caroline replies:

'Much better to economise and have one really good one.' The Saki can also read at times like a pre-emptive anticipation of the Huxley. A talker is informed of 'the great delusion of you would-be advanced satirists; you imagine you can sit down comfortably for a couple of decades saying daring and startling things about the age you live in, which, whatever other defects it may have, is certainly not standing still.' There were talkers and writers and advanced satirists of the age who subscribed to Saki's views on one contentious matter – a matter arising in *The Unbearable Bassington*, on an occasion of which he writes: 'Also in evidence, at discreet intervals, were stray units of the semitic tribe that nineteen centuries of European neglect had been unable to mislay.' You can't say that they weren't to try!

What you *can* say is that Lawrence's suspicion of such stray units is a feature of his writings, but that it is absent from Huxley's account of Lawrence in this novel. There's no collusion in the novel between Rampion and the Fascist Everard Webley, though they go to the same parties and night-clubs. Webley motors to his death through the *rus in urbe* that my father loved to paint: 'Great shafts of powdery radiance leaned down from the west between the trees and in the shadows the twilight was a mist of lavender, a mist of blue and darkening indigo, plane after plane into the hazy London distance.'

Lawrence's pamphlet of 1929, 'Pornography and Obscenity', was consulted when I first read Huxley's novel. It is less advanced than I thought then. For one thing, Master Bates receives his comeuppance there: self-abuse 'produces idiots', Lawrence writes, like any doctor of the day. And with the confidence of a certain literary critic of the day, he writes: 'The real masturbation of Englishmen began only in the nineteenth century.' After the act of self-abuse, the body remains 'a corpse', whereas sexual intercourse, even 'the homosexual intercourse', takes two, and 'something quite new is added.' The mob is blamed for scratching at its dirty little secret. Don Juans, bohemians and hygienists are blamed for their 'sex in the head', their deadly adulteries: Lawrence and Huxley were at one in an opposition to libertinage. Yeats and Shaw were at one in being bothered by the black-joke, diabolic proximity of the sexual and the excretory organs, and Lawrence has to explain that the functions are very different. 'No other civilisation has driven sex into the underworld, and nudity to the WC,' he deplores, as if speaking of two equally unsuitable places. We must come out of the closet and be open and free and nude – but not hygienic: here, in his distaste for the pursuit of health through sexual intercourse, he was at one with T. S. Eliot.

Permissives of a later date have sometimes moved to license and to advocate pornography and masturbation: Lawrence writes as if he would like to ban the damned things, and if this now seems steep, it has to be said that, in seeing them as the one damned thing, the definitions offered in his pamphlet are at some points persuasive. Pencilled into my copy, however, is a definition of Shaw's – 'a pornographic novelist is one who exploits the sex instinct as a prostitute does' – which may have struck me as more serviceable, in my search for the liberated whole man or boy. I was to find that openness has its pitfalls, and its pratfalls. The day came when I was to stand naked at the door of a room in London, inside which were some good-hearted lounging Adam-and-Eve bohemians. My plan was to enter and to hang about for a little while as if it were the most natural thing in the world. I have never been good at entries, and I took an age to cross the threshold of Eden. Last in, moreover, was first out.

The farces and defeats occasioned by the search for openness and wholeness were not to put me off the enlightenment I thought I recognised in the literature of the early years of the century and the last quarter of the previous one. From these years, which seemed like yesterday to me, came my texts and pretexts, my young men. Some of the writers I read were more evangelical, and more ideological, than others, with George Moore resplendent in the missionary position. I copied out in my diary an 'excellent' rodomontade from his autobiographical novel of 1888, *Confessions of a Young Man* – a passage in which the young man spreads the gospel of his master, Gautier. Living off his Irish rents, this young man feeds guinea pigs to his python in Paris, then moves to London to shock the bourgeoisie with his French opinions, and to brag that he regrets nothing. Moore himself was less impervious, no doubt: this is, after all, fiction – that form of words in which author and first-person narrator are understood to be different persons. But it is also a memoir, whose author sometimes purports to imagine a show-off someone else, who isn't Moore, or Moore exactly, and who even has a name of his own, though Moore can barely remember what it is. His vivid book, with its strong period interest, is now, for me, a weariness of the flesh it keeps mentioning, but there was a time when it was nothing of the kind, when it was more than faintly blissful. Moore's dawn did something for mine. In revising the novel several years later, he worked over the passage in question, cooling it a little, a very little, to produce the version that entered my diary:

> This plain scorn of a world exemplified in lacerated saints and a crucified Redeemer opened up a prospect of new beliefs and new joys in things and new revolts against all that had come to form part and parcel of the commonalty of mankind. Shelley's teaching had been, while accepting the body, to dream of the soul as a star, and so preserve our ideal; but now I saw suddenly, with delightful clearness and with intoxicating conviction, that by looking without shame and accepting with love the flesh. I might raise it to as high a place within as divine a light as even the soul had been set in. The ages were as an aureole, and I stood as if enchanted before the noble nakedness of the elder gods: not the middle nudity that sex has preserved in this modern world, but the clean pagan nude – a love of life and beauty, the broad fair breast of a boy, the long flanks, the head thrown back. I cried out with my master: the bold fearless gaze of Venus is lovelier than the lowered glance of the Virgin.

Paul Morel of *Sons and Lovers* (1913) and the Stephen Dedalus of Joyce's *Portrait* (1916) were not so much characters as authorial presences – all the better as such for adoption and impersonation. Huxley's latterday Sebastian was a character, less authorial, and a lesser light – but none the less evangelically instructive for that; the book to which he belonged had me running to the dictionary to look up the word 'homosexual'. All three writers shed light, and all three were users of the word 'radiant'. Huxley uses it for the garden city of London. Joyce uses it for Stephen's joy at the heavenly sight of the girl with kilted skirts on the beach at Howth. Lawrence uses it for the scene when Paul and Clara make love, during the night, in her mother's kitchen.

They have been to the theatre, Paul in his hard-won dinner-jacket. Lawrence has heavenly words, very simple ones too, for what happens in the kitchen. 'Then he looked at her, his face radiant . . . The hot blood came up wave upon wave. She laid her head on his shoulder.' I was untroubled by the physiology of the encounter – though my mind did stray to Hector's imitation of Grierson's quaint medical rendering, in lectures, of Wordsworth's 'felt in the blood, and felt along the heart'.

Of the books in question Lawrence's meant most, and I felt for it just what a foster-child friend of mine reported in a letter: 'I am in an emotional welter with *Sons and Lovers*. Extraordinarily affecting book. Brings out one's morbid melancholies horribly.' Both in my friend's case and in my own, this welter was partly produced by special affinities, felt in the blood, between reader and subject-matter. Like Paul, I lived among miners, and was about to leave them, and I was glad to enter a book with a scullery in it, where a dinner-jacket was a feat, and Mrs Morel's unsparing gentility a force to be reckoned with. Lawrence meant a great deal to me then, and I was interested to learn, from his *Selected Letters* of 1992, of Philip Larkin's interest in him at this same time, in the days of his youth; Larkin was also to respond to the Fulke Greville epigraph in *Point Counter Point* and to apply to himself the notion of self-division – in hopes, perhaps, of a Lawrentian cure. Both of us were to seize on one in particular of Lawrence's soothsayings: 'You live by what you thrill to.'

Mrs Morel's gentility, and Lawrence's complicity with it, were to become an objection to the novel, an objection which has focused in recent times on the treatment given to Paul's uncouth father. It could be said that the reader is allowed to know the pain there is in its diminishing of the father. And it seems to me now that there is a deeper problem, turning on a kind of favouritism. Clara, who makes Paul radiant, has been forgotten by the time he walks off quickly towards the town, having appeared to reach the end of his mother's power over him, and taken part in her death. By then, Clara has been delivered back to a husband more uncouth than miner Morel. When Mrs Morel tells Paul that Clara will not be able to hold him, we are meant to agree, and barely to mind. For the leaver, Paul, radiant Clara and his other friend Miriam, lacking in radiance, are episodes – their job in the book is, in part, to be left behind. From these orphans, consideration is withheld. Needless to say, I missed all this when I was young. I was more interested in love affairs than in what happens when they come to an end.

This 'favouritism' belongs to the self-interested art of Narcissus, who has written lots of books. One of them begins by saying that its hero is a man of 'more than common height', slow to smile and 'master of his company', who wants to be 'independent' of the world. An awareness of such favouritism, and of the need for writers to control it and correct for it, had been, as I was later to tell myself, among the determinants of genre in literature. Later still, I was to tell myself that the motive to which such favouritism attests is widely attested there, that it is no respecter of generic boundaries and can dispense with the creation of character in fiction. Those who found it in *Sons and Lovers* might find it in *The Waste Land*.

CHAPTER FIVE

Mount of Venus

'Any for Fraser?' I was asked in the December of 1947. I was delivering letters in Edinburgh's Cowgate, crouched in its ancient squalor down below George IV Bridge, where my libraries were, and had been approached by one of the city's old witches, no sister to any of the shoal of females that greeted you when you forced open the front door of Binn's department store and out like quicksilver would dart well-to-do Jeanies and Jessies in their beige and field-grey snug winter coats. 'I don't think so,' I said. 'No, definitely not.' I was looking into a blind eye that flashed a wild blue light, while the other flashed a ghastly glee. 'Definitely not?' She looked as if she'd never been sent a letter in her life. Thrawn Janet went on: 'You're not from Edinburgh. You're a London boy.' Definitely not, I told her. But she knew who she was talking to; her crone's ironies struck home. I had gone to this desolation to make some Christmas money. But I'd also gone to be sorry for the people there, and to assist them. I was a visiting angel, a boy of feeling, a Master Theresa.

'Oh to utter bloody hell with this,' said the old postman I worked with, pausing at a dark and fetid tenement landing. Elsewhere, as I climbed up one of these staircases of mine, I heard a treble voice, somewhere beneath me, singing its way, word-perfect, through the carol 'Still the Night'. Sensibility leeched onto these heavenly sounds: here, I told my diary, adoring the treble, was the real, the crone-proof messenger of light.

In general, however, Heaven was becoming more and more impalpable to me. Tommy and I spoke about it as we lay together in bed. This newspaper reader, this man of fires and crashes and footballers' suspensions *sine die*, reported that a neighbour had passed away.

'Passed away? Where to?'

'To Heaven.'

'Where's that?'

'Where's that? Ye see it every day. In the sky. Ye dinna ken your geography.'

A few days into the new year, I was dozing or lolling in the back bedroom, while Tommy sat at his slow tea in the kitchen and Granny went about her jobs. Then I heard Tom calling: 'Karl, Karl, come here quick.' My grandmother was stretched out across the kitchen fender, and there was blood on the hearth. Tom, so long looked after, was helping her to her feet – a moving sight in itself. She'd been having unmentioned dizzy spells, and now her forehead was bruised, her eye blackened, her right temple cut. There was a further cut on her hand – calloused, said the diary, by a hundred years of hard work. When she was seen by the doctor we learnt that her heart was weak. But she began to mend, to smile away her bruises, and to 'profit' by a much-needed rest. Or so I hoped as I bent my head to the pages of *Sons and Lovers*, where the *liebestod* of Mrs Morel was impending.

The first three months of 1948, shadowed by my grandmother's accident, were spent preparing for my Leaving Certificate exams, the Highers. I took time off for a somewhat impassive reading of *La Chartreuse de Parme* in French. I would sit in the sitting-room with my poems, my exercise books and my three current icons: a photograph of Canova's statue of Amor and Psyche, whose marble wings and anodyne embrace proved a disappointment – did not 'inspire me'; Picasso's *Girl before a Mirror*, a Cubist painting influenced, or so I understood, by Catalonian frescos of the Middle Ages; and a detail from the fresco by Giotto which has St Francis consorting with his birds. The last of these was to determine the choice of a peacock-blue dressing-gown, the first in a succession of such garments, in which I have long been in the habit, first thing every morning, of feeding birds that often fail to come to my crumbs. A monk's habit, for one of a small repertoire of sentimental-superstitious observances in which I try for the part of the considerate, commemorative orphan. I am not alone, of course, in feeding the birds, which could perhaps be accounted a Scottish as well as a Franciscan practice. Thomas Carlyle did it, my Aunt Peggy did it religiously, and the new leader of the Labour Party, Edinburgh's John Smith, who will receive my crumb at the next election, does it too, and did it the morning after he was chosen.

My plan was to stay on at school in the Sixth Form and to get into a university. My main subjects were Latin, Greek and English, which I was happy to treat, and to be allowed to treat, as the same subject – literature. I was as happy to read Homer and Catullus – and to do so, as best I could, in their own languages – as I was to read all but a very few English poets. Classical studies at the school were literary and linguistic in character, and there was a mistaken tendency to abstain from philosophy, and indeed from history. We heard something, but not that much, about Plato and Aristotle, while hours would go by as we forced a passage, with cutlass, compass and theodolite, through some single-sentence, page-sized undergrowth of Thucydidean syntax. Philosophy, though, would occasionally break in.

'When Plato looked at a wall,' rasped a Latin teacher one sunny morning, pointing to a specimen of the kind beyond the classroom window, to a wall which surrounded a garden accessible to Professor Grierson down the street, 'he didn't just look at the wall. What did Plato want to do when he looked at a wall?' A boy mustered the reply that 'Plato wanted to know what was on the other side.' The class laughed loudly at that, while the master was irate – the right answer having to do with essence of wall, with the ideal wall, the one laid up in heaven. It seemed that philosophy didn't care about the specimen that might at that moment have been concealing from us Herbert Grierson's morning walk, and it may also have seemed that literature was different – often disposed to appeal to those who wanted to know what was on the other side of walls.

It was a good school, but there was a fair amount that it did not teach. Finance, law, medicine, the processes of government, among other aspects of the practical and professional life of the country, were missing from the curriculum. But it was pretty much my own fault that when I went to work at the Treasury, I had still to learn what Bank Rate was, and the difference between a rate and a rent.

In April, when the exams were over, I descended to London to visit my father and the Berks – Lotte and Ernest and their fourteen-year-old daughter, Esther. It was there that I received the news that I would never see my grandmother again. She had fallen ill with pneumonia after my departure. 'The person whom I loved most in all the world is dead.' These child-like words were written in my journal as her body lay in its coffin in the front bedroom: 'Georgina B. Y. Connor, died 9th April 1948. Aged 79.' The 'B. Y.' referred to her maiden names, Buchan Young, and, you could say, to the ploughlands to the south of Jeanie Deans' wood, where she was born; in later years, I would wear a Buchanan tartan tie, as a kind of favour – when I wasn't feeding the birds, as it were.

Down in London I'd been told by letter that she was ill, and told to stay where I was for the time being. She had said to her daughters: 'Illness frichts him. Let him enjoy himself while he is still young.' Illness frightens me all right, but it seemed to me that I should not have been kept away, that I'd been punished for enjoying myself. I was 'pained with a thousand thoughts and a thousand wonderings', among them the question of what would happen to me now. Such thoughts, confided to my journal, caused me to feel repelled by its farrago of 'Victorian platitude' and 'pseudo-modern maunderings'. It had to change, to become more of a writer's notebook.

The funeral was held on 15 April. 'This corruptible shall put on incorruption,' declared the minister – offensively, I found – in the sitting-room. In Liberton kirkyard Bob walked to the grave, taking his brother Tom by the hand, Tom hunched and awkward, his face screwed up in a Scots rictus, his limbs enclosed, no doubt, in one of his brother's business suits. They were like father and son. Afterwards I had a talk with Bob. I could be offered to my parents – in two pieces, presumably, as in the judgement of Solomon – or to one or the other. But it was accepted that I was now in a position to decide for myself. 'I shall stay here,' I decided.

Staying here, I also began to stay there – travelling to London to resemble the young Werther in Shepherd's Bush, where Lotte was deemed 'terrifically beautiful, witty, *spirituelle*, intellectual', and yet 'kind and natural', and where she was to notice that I had a body that resembled a noodle. Her dancing days were almost over, and there were times when she seemed unsettled, or becalmed, at a loss for what to do next with all her energy and comic verve. But Lotte's calms were more interesting than the next person's storms. Art and love and Europe were apparent in Shepherd's Bush, where books and plays and paintings were exclaimed about as 'vunderful'. Lotte had recently sold Orson Welles's Harry Lime a ticket to the Ferris wheel, at the climax of the film *The Third Man*, in which a crooked post-war Europe was evoked. I went to the pictures and pored like a *cinéaste* over the footage, the frames, in question.

These wonders might have made Scotland look a dark shade of grey. But Scotland had its writers and artists too, and its girls. One girl was called Louise and came from Leith: Louise was a contentless, sequel-less moment of accord among the dunes and tussocks of Port Seton as we sat like sand castles in the unaccustomed heat looking up at a tall Larkin sky, charged with an azure light and the promise, as it felt, of escape, or extinction. My family remained important, dear to me, even though I was now able to orphan myself into imagining, for a while, that I had found another family in London, where the thought was returned and I was welcomed by people who had even less money to spare than there was at Gilmerton. I was often to visit my ain folk in later years, fearing that I had left them to their quiet ways, which were also their quarrelsome ways. Miller went back to Connor because I wanted to see them and because I taxed myself with deserting them. It then became clear that I wanted to go back to Scotland in a way I hadn't foreseen. By the Seventies, when I spent the summers in a cottage near Berwick, dualistically suspended between North and South, I had discovered that I wished to think and write about Scottish writers and the Scottish past. I went to live, for spells, not only in Berwickshire but in the Edinburghs of 1630 and 1800.

Walter Scott proclaims my part of Midlothian in one of the rhetorical questions which he liked to ask:

> Who knows not Melville's beechy grove,
>   And Roslin's rocky glen,
> Dalkeith, which all the virtues love,
>   And classic Hawthornden?

I knew about them, and was to put them into books. Henry Cockburn, about whom I wrote, wrote about Lord Melville – his uncle by marriage, the politician Henry Dundas – and about the Dundases' great house of Arniston, a mile or so from Gilmerton, where the name meant only the nearby mining village when I was a boy; and I shall presently be writing in this book about my lifelong intermittent interest in the poet William Drummond of Hawthornden. Dalkeith was the not especially virtuous town where I bought my Utility bicycle during the war, a bike which certainly possessed the native merit of solidity and on which, bone-shaken and saddle-sore, I toiled from one youth hostel to another. These rural rides were remembered in a confessional remark to my Aunt Peggy: 'I need love as a bike needs oil.'

Landscapes, which were often Scottish, came to matter to me in much the way that I imagine they must have done to Norman MacCaig and Andrew Young; there were those that were to lodge in my head like the jewel in that of Young's toad. The map of Midlothian's bonny bits and seaward sweep spreads out before you if you station yourself on the high ground above Dalkeith and turn your face towards Edinburgh; distance lends enchantment and the foul toad of its sore spots is barely detectable. It is all much as it must once have been. From Hawthornden, which lies inland to the left, the Esk runs down to Lasswade, where Scott lived when he was first married and where Thomas De Quincey lived on towards an advanced old age with the constitution of a MacDiarmid, an enduring drug dependency and a phantasmagoric literary production. My grandmother's birthplace and Jeanie Deans' wood are not far off. Over towards the Pentlands are the village of Straiton and

Loanhead pit, where my Irish grandfather, Robert Connor, wrought, or wrocht, as his wife would say, as a checkweighman. He was also a trade-unionist and a fiddler, and by all accounts something of a caution and a tease. He once went to London to represent his union and took time off to go to a concert hall to listen to Heifetz play the violin; one of Heifetz's strings broke and Robert Connor was reputed to have supplied him with a spare. None of his children, except for my mother, was to pursue his politics; his daughter Peggy was attached to the Border premier Lord Home.

Over beyond the city, by the sea, where Portobello Pool once splashed and yelled, stands Portobello Prom, along which my mother and I walked in procession with her Communist friends, the men in open-necked shirts and navy-blue serge suits, with Red Star lapel badges. The time for these reds to be swept under the bed had not yet arrived: the view from Dalkeith reminds me of the occasion when my mother and I encountered the Communist intelligentsia, in the persons of an Edinburgh University lecturer and his wife, together with some like minds, in an open-plan modern house, set with its face to the future – a future that could be about to work – on a Pentlands foothill.

The pits are gone now, or going, from the Midlothian panorama. Staying not long ago at Drummond's little castle of Hawthornden, which has become a writers' retreat, I paid a visit to Rosewell, remembered as a fragrant Alain-Fournier-like mysterious place-name on the front of buses, and found a ghost town, with not a soul in the street and a few male souls drinking and betting their doles at two in the afternoon in their miners' retreat – a saloon the size of a baronial hall.

There is no better picture of the Edinburgh of my schooldays than Muriel Spark's novel *The Prime of Miss Jean Brodie*, which is about the Edinburgh of ten years before. This testifies, I think, to the importance of schools for the generations in question, and to the history of their mattering in this part of the world. Scotland's classic works are more likely than those of most other countries to include such a title as *My Schools and Schoolmasters* – by the, as it happens, mostly self-taught Hugh Miller, who was to hew his mason's stones, for a while, within sight of Craigmillar Castle, among colliers who had been born slaves in the earlier eighteenth century.

This novel by the expatriate Spark has by heart the heart of Midlothian. It dances from Morningside and Merchiston, and Bruntsfield Links, where she grew up, to 'the reeking network of slums which the Old Town constituted in those years . . . a misty region of crime and desperation', then down for its Saturday afternoons to the Forth estuary at Cramond, where I, too, went for walks. I was born around 'the first anniversary of the launching of Miss Brodie's prime', Miss Brodie being the Hector MacIver of her favourite class, the 'crème de la crème'. These girls attend a school modelled on James Gillespie's, and they are alive, in a period sense no less beguiling at the Royal High, to 'the sexual significance of everything', which may be thought a near-reprise of Hogg's 'sexual intercourse of things'. It is possible to catch, in Spark's writings, the note of a Lothian language which could be heard uttering and coining over the decades. This language contributes to the nostalgic appeal of her memoir of 1992, *Curriculum Vitae*, which is at its best in recalling the Edinburgh of the Thirties and which identifies Jean Brodie's original in Miss Christina Kay of Gillespie's, and in which she cites someone's version of the 'many are cauld' Biblical word-play I reckoned I'd invented: the version she cites refers to a breakdown in the heating system of a Scottish office.

Miss Brodie has a love affair with the art teacher and a sex affair with the music teacher, and her girls imagine her yielding to the latter in a style which came to me as no surprise: 'They placed Miss Brodie on the lofty lion's back of Arthur's Seat, with only the sky for roof and bracken for a bed.' I then read in *Curriculum Vitae* that the art teacher had an original in 'dishy Arthur Couling', fancied by Muriel Spark at Gillespie's, from which he moved to teach me art at the Royal High. The snapshot remains in my head of a haystack of his on show among the paintings at the Royal Scottish Academy. I went to admire it, not imagining that Arthur had ever been a dish, or that his seat might one day serve, together with that of an imaginary colleague, as an object of contemplation for a set of imaginary girls. For me, as for these girls, Arthur's Seat was a Mount of Venus. Half-way up Arthur's Seat I'd listened to Ernest's good news, and, before that, to a faintly chilling slick blond piper in the school's Army Training Corps band, who lay in his regalia in the bracken, adjusting his sporran as he ran his hand over a patch of wind-punished grass, while informing me that this was what a woman's pubic hair was like. Thank God, I may have felt, it wasn't like a sporran.

In the language of the native theology which Muriel Spark refused to accept, you could say that *The Prime of Miss Jean Brodie* is the book which she was destined to write. Miss Christina Kay is commemorated in it, with many of her traits intact: the mastery of her class, the Fascist sympathies, the art worship, the dark complexion, the moustache. What, then, are the differences? 'The sexual significance of everything', which so diverts the girls in the novel, has its epicentre in Miss Brodie: but Miss Kay would appear to have been as innocent as Arthur Couling no doubt was of participation in the kind of sexual scene ascribed to her. Unlike Miss Brodie, moreover, she was a devout Protestant. The Reformed religion was largely withheld from a novel in which history and geography might have conspired to locate it, and sex and Catholicism rushed in to fill the vacuum. Having been awarded a sex affair with the art teacher, and having betrayed her mentor in the matter of these Fascist sympathies, Sandy of the narrow little eyes is pent behind bars in the narrow cell of a nunnery. Sandy's betrayal is neither trivial nor endearing, and it is likely to be, for some readers of the novel, an enigma. More in the manner of the Calvinist God, who hath done whatsoever He hath pleased, than in the explaining manner of most novelists, Muriel Spark must have willed it that way, must have been pleased with it: but her readers may well have wondered what she meant by Sandy's betrayal and retreat.

She has often been interested in betrayal, and Sandy's may have given expression to feelings that included a highly-charged sense of departure from the Edinburgh of her Scottish and

Jewish forebears. There are those, as I was to find myself, for whom there is nothing trivial about even the most sensible of such departures. Job-seeking, and Scottish-looking, while still in Scotland after leaving school, she firmly presented herself as the possessor of a Jewish name, and she was moved by some of the observances of the faith. But her former friend Derek Stanford's memoir of 1977, *Inside the Forties*, speaks of her, not implausibly, as having placed a distance between herself and Jewishness. Like Walter Scott, with his own ambivalence on the subject, she was later to be plagued by a Jewish businessman – in New York, when Stanford got round to betraying her by selling the letters she had sent him.

Spark's buoyant novel requires an effort of interpretation – an effort which her memoir, *Curriculum Vitae*, does not make. It says less than the novel does, for instance, about why the name Brodie was adopted. The memoir mentions an American family friend of that name, while Miss Brodie herself claims descent from the famous eighteenth-century burglar and double-liver, Deacon Brodie. This is one of the sinister meanings which she attracts and which make her betrayable.

Unlike Miss Brodie, Hector did not seek to control or indoctrinate his pupils. He was not the author of our being. We were not the novel he was writing. But for those who became his friends he was an education and a wonder. The letters I was to receive in the four or five years that followed, from Hector, Norman MacCaig, Robert Taubman, Paul Harper and others, are chastening, when I reread them now, in the interest they take and the interest they afford. 'If there are any books you would like and can't get, I'll be glad to be your agent,' wrote Norman when I was in the Army, at a time when Peggy was writing nutritious letters too, besides washing my pyjamas for me and parcelling them back across the Rhine. Keen on horse-racing and on aeroplanes ('lovely slim things'), Paul Harper of the long nails and bloodless face had more of a flair for writing than any other boy of our age at the school, and a flair for crisis which did not desert him with the end of adolescence. These were literary rather than ideological people, in the manner of the

73

Fifties that were about to unfold, and they were all excellent advertisements for friendship.

Each of Hector's letters was a performance, executed with panache, richly-phrased and hung with quotations from *Macbeth*. Werthering in London, I heard from him about an Edinburgh 'welter' – a word some of our set seemed intent on adding to the Lothian lingo – which had occurred at the Freemasons' Hall, on one of the city's civic occasions, and which co-starred a very important person and a rising schoolfellow of mine, Walter Dickson – as Hector phrased it,

> the Right Honourable Walter Elliot and the Left Honourable Walter Dickson. The de la Mares and Pidgeons were otherwise engaged. Walter Elliot talked for the greater part of an hour on the World we Want. His speech was a bit of Border tweed with a clear, almost piercing pattern for the buyers but no pulsating colours and no thickness of texture. Besides he infuriated me by using phrases he had previously used in the Sunday papers. Nevertheless, sweet Tweed ran softly till he sang his song. I did chairman at one of the discussion groups. After that I went away. I was tired of waltering in the welter of it all.

Later, in 1952, from a 'noisy, squalid pub', the Ivanhoe, he wrote to say that he'd prevailed on the barman to let him listen to a discussion I was chairing on the Light Programme of the BBC. A practical criticism ensued, somewhat obstructed by the attentions of a prostitute opposite, the one with 'the red head-scarf and the circular green brooch and the sunken off-agate eyes', who kept asking him for a light.

A letter of Norman's, in 1950, deals with another civic occasion, this time the hosting of a PEN Congress. It opens with the news that 'the writing chiels are all very silent. I mean the young ones, not the lime-lit ones.' So-and-so is 'still dumb, except for a very, very few bad lyrics'. Somebody else 'still stabs himself to death in every paper one picks up and most broadcasts. I myself trickle away in my usual purely medicinal manner.' The Congress had contained 'lamentable expositions of damn-all, only enlivened when the air was filled with lopsided characters lumbering about on their one, Left wing'. But there was more to Edinburgh than displays of this sort, more to it than its Lord Provost: 'May his guts fall out.' He apologises for painting the place in 'soot and charcoal. You are right in finding something here that is a special thing to all Scots and has some meaning, surely, for others. It is, anyway, a place I would never leave.' It is a place which his letters describe almost as well as his poems. Of its 'wild wind and wild wet' he writes: 'life tries to make itself consist of streaming shop-windows, mad tramcars, women half-jelled in plastic capes and pixies, and all the tiny blasted heaths of front gardens populated with demented Lears throwing their branches all airts and saying "Spout".'

In 1951 he threw a storm of his own on the subject of Ezra Pound's *Letters*:

> a fatuous and dull book by a fatuous and interesting man, who seems too like a lesser and Yankee MacDiarmid for it to be possible. He likes words the way a cannibal likes missionaries, but he shouldn't spit his gobbets and shreds into a book. Hardly a word emerges from this one without its tongue twisted round its neck and wearing its kneecap for a monocle. He's a horror, a nasty little four-years-old horror who picks the wings off nouns and burns beautiful wriggling adjectives in tin lids of methylated spirits. And knows Chinese. And knows damn-all. And doesn't know it.

This example of Norman thunderously at play – comically heated for the cheering-up of a conscript – reads like an augury of the flytings due to be let fly by young English writers of the Movement school in the course of the next decade.

Robert Taubman's letters, while just as encouraging, were never heated. They were those of an Existentialist who was apt in closing to wish you 'a reasonably good summer'; his own discouragements were examined with an austere candour, and clothed in the manners of a gentleman. He was indeed English – Manx – as well as Edinburgh, and had barely left the Royal High when he found himself serving as an Indian Army colonel in the jungle war against the Japanese. After that, he had taken a degree at Edinburgh and wandered around what Hector called 'the countries of the South Wind' – Italy and France. He went on to be a university administrator, a good if infrequent literary critic, a married man and a father, and is now, for all the world, a retired colonel in his seventies. But at the time of these letters, casting about for a job, falling in love, he was capable of writing: 'Quite clearly, my life is at an end; I ought at least to be sitting in a café jabbing a knife into my hand, like the existentialists.' This was a dry joke – and where there are semi-colons there's hope. But he was a serious reader of Sartre, who could talk of wanting to write an English Existentialist novel. There was something of Sartre, as well as something of Eliot's 'escape from personality' and of Lawrence's meditated destruction of 'the old stable ego' of the fictional character, in Rob's idea of how two people might get on together: an idea in which romantic friendship was both abolished and reconstituted. He didn't want to think of me, he wrote,

only as a special kind of object – a person. I know people say one should always be conscious of someone else as a person. But that seems to me to put a distance between the two – one feels judged and constrained by the presence of the other. In fact, I feel free with you, as if no kind of constraint, no awareness of you as another person, were there. A sort of impersonal communion, with the individual personalities withdrawn to vanishing-point: I suppose that's what I mean by sharing experience. Of course that generally happens when our conversation is at its silliest, rather than when an important argument is going on. And it seemed that there isn't perhaps a great range of actual experience that we do want to share, or can share, unfortunately. There's also the fact that you are naturally, I think, a more self-sufficient person than me, and probably less inclined to abandon your own resources for anything outside yourself (I remember that the girl Ivich in the *The Age of Reason* used to remind me of you – no doubt quite unjustly): you may deny this, but don't deny it because you think I'm more capable of coping with railway trains and timetables than you – that, if it's true at all, is only because I've more need to build up an objective, practical self in order to exist at all. But this distinction of personalities is just what I wanted to avoid: it is the enemy of freedom between us.

I was all for personality myself, though not in theory opposed to communion, and saw this, egotistically, as a snub inflicted on an effusive egotist by an embodiment of English reserve. The idea he was developing led on to what appeared to me to be an endorsement, on his part, of Samuel Johnson's observation that a man 'should keep his friendship in constant repair': you had to keep adding to your friends. I didn't like the disloyal sound of that. I have suffered a few subtractions since – but Rob remains. I hope he has a reasonably good summer.

I am getting ahead of myself here, though, and would like to return to the point where most of these friendships began, and where I began in earnest to stretch my legs and write plays and stories. Together with a school friend, I dashed off a play, *The Authors of Mischief*, which, in July 1948, was put on in the Junior School at Jock's Lodge, near Portobello Pool. 'My very bones are squealing under the strain' – it was still being written when Hector set to work to shore it up in production. The collaboration between the two authors brought much of the mischief that collaboration is noted for, and a mess was made of a promising theme.

The play was based on a student revolt of the sixteenth century, when the boys of the High School of the time – a school which threatened, in terms not unfamiliar to us, to chastise 'the disobedient, gamblers, those who come to school late in the morning, those who have not prepared their lesson, those speaking in the vernacular tongue and the authors of mischief' – were denied a holiday. They then barricaded themselves in and shot the bailie who came with a posse to disperse them. In the words of a contemporary chronicler, 'they ramforcit the doors of the said scooll, swa that thai refusit to lat in thair

77

Maistir nor na wthir man, without thai wer grantit thair priviledge conforme to thair wountit use . . . Thair came ane scoller callit William Sinklar . . . and with ane pistollet schot the said Baillie throw the heid.' The ringleader, William Sinclair, son of the Earl of Caithness, was presented as a fascist demagogue, his victim Bailie MacMoran as a bullying bore, and the headmaster Hercules Rollock, a writer of Latin verse, as the schoolboy's friend and as the decent man in the affair, which ended, as in fact, with the boys' expulsion and arrest. To supply pathos, a wee boy was invented, Gideon Hortensius Bannerman, who pines to quit the siege and go home to his mother for a jam piece. The poet Drummond, who is likely to have been one of the pupils of the school at the time, 1595, was overlooked.

I'd like to feel that our play had foretastes of the Sixties, with their events of May, their sit-ins and their teach-ins, their burnings of books, their imagination-takes-power, their tigers of wrath which are wiser than the horses of instruction. But there is probably more in the play of Hitler's seizure of power in Germany, not that very long before. Such wrath as there is is aimed at noblemen and bossy bailies, and the instructor is a good egg, which looks like a compliment or a deference to the High School teachers who were sitting in the audience. 'Everything imaginable has been happening these last few days when you were away in Falkirk,' bumbles a bailie. Into this chatter are spliced choric verse passages modelled on the Eliot and the Auden and Isherwood poem-play. The only bit I can now bear comes when, after the murder, a boy raises his eyes to the horizon and says: 'It's been a wonderful day – look, you can see the Pentlands quite clearly across the houses and the fields.' But then another boy has to say: 'There's one man that won't be seeing the Pentlands again.'

In August I went abroad for the first time, to see Paris, as one of a party of schoolchildren. We stayed in a hostel where our guide was spruce Marcel, a Spanish lawyer and Communist, a reciter of the poetry of Lorca which Ernest used to dance and Norman and I stand at the Post Office discussing. He was also an acquaintance of Maurois and Utrillo and a friend of Sartre.

'But he does not absolutely subscribe to the theory of Existential-ism.' I was not long in learning that he was a subscriber to the seduction of girls. 'It's strange how some men can have the loosest relations with women personally, and yet entertain the narrowest of views on sex as a larger phenomenon in life.' He showed me snaps of fifteen girls who had been his mistresses in the previous year, and I was to glimpse him through a window as he made his way across his room towards No 16 on the *catalogo questo*. Homosexuality, however, repelled him – it was the 'conjunction of two similarly-formed organs' that put him off. But it did not put him off lesbianism – or, for that matter, Lorca. One night the party attended a performance of *Boris Godunov*, where Marcel held the left breast of one of our lassies as our Scots faces glowered at the stage: he remarked that he'd never enjoyed an opera so much in all his life. There is a story of this date about a Lallans poet who leant wildly out of a Paris taxi to wave at the women, and was ordered by his wife to 'stop it at once. You're not in Edinburgh now.' At the hostel, we were entirely convinced that we were in Paris.

Don Juan and his exploits gave way to Winchelsea, where the Berks were on holiday, and I went back with them to London, to their penthouse flat at the summit of a block called The Grampians, in Shepherd's Bush. 'This here is your home too,' said Lotte. When the weather was fine, we would sleep (Lotte-less) cuddled up in our makeshift beds on the roof, beneath the stars. The weather always seemed to be fine, with London's skies a permanent Port Seton blue. There was magic in the very smuts that drifted down onto sills and parapets and wash-basins, in those days when London landscapes could still be green but when the law had yet to rule that the air be clean. I was happy. It was as if the Pentlands had been freighted to King's Cross and piled, Pelion on Ossa, all over The Grampians.

In the course of my last year at school, September 1948 to June 1949, I did three pieces of writing: a radio play, *Damon in Albany*, about my neighbour Drummond of Hawthornden, a story, 'The Nether Fields', and a verse satire – a parody of Dylan Thomas's *Eighteen Poems* – on some innovations devised

79

by the rector of the school. I was eventually offered bursaries at Edinburgh University, in English and in Classics, and a place to read English at Downing College, Cambridge, under F. R. Leavis. Robert Taubman interested me in Leavis and coached me for the exam, and it was to Cambridge that I chose to go. 'You had better become word-perfect in your Eliot,' said Rob later, correcting a misquotation, 'before you enter the community of Little Downing.'

When I went down there that autumn to sit the scholarship exam, I might have reflected that my life had been, and would continue to be, laid end to end with exams. Except for the ones I couldn't do, I found them exciting; it was like being in a race; and I never found that the discipline of exams was to spoil the studies I took to. At the same time, they were an anxiety which weighed on a student for a third of his life. As a retired professor, I still dream of sitting them and of a force, a hidden hand, that prevents me from doing so. When the time came, there could be tantrums and symptoms. At this point, in 1948, a whine began in my left ear, like the noise you hear from your Toshiba or from a descending aircraft, and it was with difficulty that I reached the decision to stop listening to it. It is still there. The thing, as so often, is to stop listening. When I set off to have my adenoids out, still squeamish from a hernia operation of several years before, I was reduced to fortitude by the information that Taubman had had his out on a kitchen table.

During the autumn I was one of a team which took part in BBC Radio's *Top of the Form* quiz competition. The quizmaster was Lionel Gamlin, a star broadcaster and Pathé newscaster, and a star recaller of his days at Cambridge, with their elocutionary Union, and their Footlights and Amateur Dramatic Club, where much of the national theatre of later days was presently to originate. He had large ears which my father would have pressed him to sleep on. I liked him. When I sent him a copy of *Schola Regia*, which I was editing, he wrote to say of a mention he'd received there: 'Thank you for the honey-sweet publicity.' When his star set with the advent of television, he took a job near Brighton as some man's Jeeves – at about the time, I suppose, when the beach was alleged to have been blotted out by copies of *Hemlock and After*. In Angus Wilson's fictions, as seldom before, homosexual lives were being frankly described, and there were excitements on that score.

I read Charles Morgan's novel *The Fountain*, published in 1932, which has that cherished hero – referred to earlier – of more than common height. According to my journal, 'it alludes to important metaphysical problems, but his treatment of them is not important, and the book is in a way trivial.' And I read Kafka with delight. My copy of *The Castle* bears Lotte's possibly ominous inscription: 'Those are pearls that were his eyes.'

Neither Lotte nor I, readers of T. S. Eliot, neither of us word-perfect, could then have known what Eliot had done with this line. He had turned it into 'That is lace that was his nose.' His poem 'Dirge', an early poem which was published after his death, uses Ariel's song in *The Tempest* while going on about the dead body of a Jew, eaten by crabs at the bottom of the sea – creatures that might have reminded me of 'the crabs of unbelief' fastened to me by a friend in the school magazine. Eliot's readers were at this time rarely disturbed, at any rate in public, by the injurious treatment which this same Bleistein had received in the published works; by some of those who *were* disturbed, presumably, the 'liberal' forbearance he liked to deprecate was exercised in his favour; an exegetical subtlety was also exercised in his favour. In a draft of the poem the word 'man' appears instead of 'Jew', and there are other such indications, elsewhere in his poetry, that Eliot was his own Jew, that the Jew could serve him both as a type of the distressed human being and as a figure for some distressing part of his nature – wandering, free-thinking, heretical, frightful. But this does not mean that his nature could not tolerate the familiar simplex anti-semite who when he thought about Jews thought about noses and gold. The discouraging ironies that can be found here are not confined to what Eliot thought and wrote on these occasions: they must also have been present, at this time, for those who chose to look, in the docility of his readers.

In February there arrived the idea for 'The Nether Fields', a title in which death and a place called Nether Liberton were joined. A wounded British soldier studies a French boy who is unable to understand his appeals for help, and the story ends with the words: 'I died.' I was that soldier, and I was the boy too. The boy who wrote the story was dying into adult life, but in the story it is the adult who dies. It is about adolescence and about failures of communication, and it would also seem to be trying to muster a response to the Taubman doctrine of impersonality and the friendship of rotary repair. Norman MacCaig thought that it was a story which was attempting to do what poems do.

I was carrying this text, to read to friends, when I fell on my face at the corner of Moredun Park Gardens, underneath the old parliamentary lamp-post – betrayed by the fringed tongues of my brogues. I ate the inside of my face, and, as it were, my words. I was led back by an AA man to my two main aunts, who were not speaking to each other at the time, and who directed looks in which alarm was tinged with distaste: perhaps I had shown myself up by falling down in the street. In doing so, I had become the dying soldier of the story. I caught flu and it took me a number of days to get back from the dead, days during which my blood remained on the pavement until the rain washed it away. I used to go and examine it. Would flowers spring up?

Elsewhere, flowers were springing up in profusion. My irons were all in the fire. Even at the time – when, after years of repining and aloning, I had added to my icons the blue boy of Picasso who clasps a dove and is clad in a nightie – I felt I was having the time of my life. On 6 April, a year, almost to the day, after my grandmother's death, I travelled down to Cambridge with Lotte, to see Leavis for a talk about my studies, which were due to happen after two years of National Service. He had written me a civil letter: 'You would find me at Downing (if you send me word that you can conveniently manage that time).'

On the train, sunk down on dusty old sagging cushions in our corner seats, Lotte and I spoke of our attachment to one another. I was as weak as could be when I got off the train. We made our way to the gates of Downing, where – I hope in candour, meaning to show her what I was – I gave her my terrible diary to read in a terrible tearoom, while I entered the college, at five p.m. sharp, for my chat.

Leavis seemed to be wearing pyjamas – it may have been the effect of his customary Shelleyan open-necked shirt. And he seemed sad. Those sombre gypsy eyes. He had the brown face bestowed by his jogs, and his forehead was scratched, as if he had thrust it through brambles to come and advise me. His lips were moist – the target for a kiss, as a poem by Stephen Spender once said (of someone else). I went back to the tearoom, to unlock Lotte from my diary.

'I am bound to put down all my moods': that diary was now trembling with phrases and snatches with which the noodle celebrated his ardent state. 'He was on her body as a bee moves and edges over a blossom.' In their midst were accounts of a trip made with Alec Kelly to Galloway, during which we encountered a stammering raconteur whose stories were drawn to the consonants he couldn't pronounce, a landlord who was always drunk, and Sweetheart Abbey – alias Dulcecor. It seemed like a forgotten countryside, with Dulcecor a drowned cathedral. I felt as if I'd stepped into the past, which is how I had felt on a cycle ride to the Burns country not far to the north. At the end of the month I embarked on the radio play about Drummond. Hector was to interest a BBC producer in the script; after long delays, in the manner of producers, this man cried off, without letting me know. Still, it had been a pleasure to write it, and it enabled me to be seconded to Army Radio when I became a conscript.

Late in June, I sat with Hector, in Grierson's leafy library, pasting up the school magazine for the last time – but it was the kind of thing I'd be doing for the rest of my life, my kind of thing. 'The difficulties and the irritations, and the offences we have given and are about to give, can't be counted,' I lied in my diary. I was still on my high. 'Everything is in an unimaginable turmoil of excitement, all my plans and their execution are humming like looms.' My last magazine carried an unctuous editorial on what it was to leave school. Auden was quoted: 'There must be sorrow if there can be love.' The same sentiments, those of a good boy, were delivered in the dux's valedictory speech at the school prizegiving. Elsewhere in the magazine I published, anonymously, my bad boy's parody of Dylan Thomas, about a staff code whereby masters lost their names and became, in regimental style, syllables and initials of the subjects they professed. The headmaster was offended by a blasphemy in the last line, and there were confabulations over that. Hector and his rector were on the brink of a quarrel which ran and ran, reminiscent of the one in Muriel Spark's novel, and which was to saddle him with a wasteful preoccupation.

From his 'bard's bothy' in Wales, Dylan Thomas responded to the poem – dispatched by Hector – with no sign of rancour (it can only have been at least a little irritating) and with the suggestion that someone had been drinking whisky. He suspected that Hector had had a finger or more in the parody. His suggestion, a teetotaller might imagine, was in the nature of a literary reference. *Letters from Iceland*, by Auden and MacNeice, had concluded with their 'Last Will and Testament', in which MacNeice bequeaths to Hector, and to Guy Burgess, 'a keg of whisky, the sweet deceiver'. MacDiarmid is bequeathed, by both authors, 'a gallon of Red Biddy'.

This effort of mine was a cut above involuntary parodies of Thomas which I'd published in the past, one of them a sonnet, a tribute to Lotte's daughter.

> This night of nights my smocked and sandalled love
> I saw go through the starlight, while on high
> My limbs grew into knives, I bled my light
> And throbbed my spouting lustres through the sky.
>
> Then I, a star, watched her come entering
> My nightly land of dazzling wounds. The dark
> Shrank from her tear as from my blazing limbs;
> She moved and loved as simple as the ark.

I was an angry, wounded star here, and after frightening off a wholesome venturer, I came to grief, as stars do in poems, and in diaries, and as the star does in the fine sonnet by Drummond which shone its light on my last days as a schoolboy and, together with Thomas's highly infectious and melodic youthful reveries and rants, helped me to write this schoolboy poem. Drummond's sonnet begins:

> As, in a dusky and tempestuous night,
> A star is wont to spread her locks of gold,
> And while her pleasant rays abroad are roll'd,
> Some spiteful cloud doth rob us of her sight . . .

Young readers rush in and emulate – embarrassing of them, but there you are. What Hugh Miller says of himself in his autobiography, published in 1854, could also have been said of me: 'with the rashness natural to immature youth, I had at this time the temerity to term myself "poet".' Sandy Brown and his bad friends at school would have had no time for these 'starry blethers' of mine, in MacDiarmid's expression, or for valedictory speeches about sorrow and love. But they might not have minded my carry-on about the staff code. It starts:

> Light breaks where there's no staff, where there's no
>   school
> Windy instruction dawns within the skull
> Of boys alone,
> And broken hearts with tickets in their hands
> File into lunch where no staff picks the bones.
>
> We've no more masters left us, only vowels;
> To passwords capped and gowned belong the tawse.
> With vatic howl,
> In the earth like bones our former ways and days
> We bury wept with pickaxes and trowels.

And it blasphemously finishes:

> How can we hope to disemvowel the staff
> Or prove such sentences not consonant
> With such a school,

Where there's no men but only syllables
And such semantic rages are the rule?

Darkness descends where J and R and G
Profess Maths, English and Geography;
Alas we find
That though in the beginning was the word
The word split up in portions is the end.

I went to Florence in the summer to stay with Robert Taubman; we were then to go off for a short walk in the Alps. I felt that I needed a rest after all I'd been through, and had regressed to jokes about my 'motherless-childlike troubles'. Rob was sent a letter in July which said: 'It's a pity that one must stand in for Atlas in order to visit one's friends.' Drummond accompanied me to Italy in the shape of his collected works, which produced total arrest in the station of Aosta in an Alpine valley. The sun beat down. In my Edinburgh man's black winter overcoat I tried to haul my loaded suitcase out of the station. It refused to budge, and I had to be helped out. I was less self-sufficient than Rob had kindly proposed. Soon afterwards I strode across a meadow towards a path which turned out to be a fifty-mile-an-hour ice-brook. I disappeared up to the tip of my nose. Above me towered my companion. Had he known about it then, he might have availed himself of a family motto of the painter he was to marry, Mary Edmond, and exhorted me in his English accent to 'haud on'. I had not enhanced his reasonably good summer.

The evening after the magazine paste-up I had sat perched on the Castle Rock in Edinburgh with a girl I scarcely knew, who startled me by saying in so many words that she wanted me to walk out with her or never to see her again. I never saw her again, but her words made me think about the restless search for partners among the young people with whom I grew up. She told me that Sheena had embraced her future husband a week after my courtship had ceased, to the music of the school choir. To this information my diary applied the Latin dictum, *Amantium irae redintegratio amoris*, twisting it to tender Johnson's advice that a man should keep his friendship in constant repair. 'The falling out of faithful friends renewing is of love' was made to mean that after a quarrel you moved on to someone else.

The constant repair of the sexual friendships of those days was more treacherous and unfeeling than I realised at the time, and I wish I had shown more consideration and more sense. It was well understood that adolescent loves don't last. But the invitations to the dance that were always being issued would lead, as often as not, to an ordeal of cross-purposes, self-deception and betrayal, with the girls expecting more in the way of fidelity than their partners, and suffering more. Juans, and 'Johnsons', suffered too, of course. They had to suffer their imbibed hostility to the ladies on the list, and to do without their friendship. It was all a welter.

Lotte was the foreign woman, or the older woman, whom outcasts have been known to desire, and whom valedictory speakers and many others have been known to desire. I was never to fall out with her. I was to feel that I should have given her more, but was never sure, lost between son and lover, as some might think, what more there might be. She went on to live a further brilliant life, as the empress of a pair of dance and aerobics places. Sometimes I stand outside Stamford Bridge Football Ground and look at the Lotte shop there, with her name in italic letters above the door. My spirit crosses the street, goes inside the midnight black of the shop window and dances with the boss.

CHAPTER SIX

Damon in Albany

Writers complain. It is expected of them, and of their sonnets especially. In this narrow space they fret profusely, while fretting not, we have been told, at the sonnet form itself. Few sonneteers, however, few writers of any sort, can have complained more insistently than William Drummond of Hawthornden. This complainer was born in 1585, and was – with such energy! – to rue the day:

> What cruel star into this world me brought?
> What gloomy day did dawn to give me light?
> What unkind hand to nurse me (orphan) sought,
> And would not leave me in eternal night?

Drummond was the ultimate naiad of the ice-brook, up to his nose in the aboriginal calamitous worst of the human condition. Next to the cradle stood the coffin: such was the sonnet shortness of the earthly life, and the earthly life was a bad business. He held that man was 'a finite piece of reasonable misery'. There was every reason but that of consistency to hope, as he also did in certain moods and at certain seasons, for translation to an eternal home at the end of it all.

His sonnets are charged with woes and mishaps, with the cries of a 'disastered Me'. They are like some of the diaries people write, like the diaries that I wrote during my adolescence. When I read him at school it was like looking in a mirror. I wasn't altogether pleased with what l saw – with all there was of the moping belletrist, the smoothly self-rehearsing specialist in misfortune, to be found in his verse. Surely this was a distorting mirror. But he became my chum, and I wrote a radio play about him. It has been interesting to compare the portrait furnished in the play with what I was to learn about him later. Drummond studies, as known to me then, consisted chiefly of the brief life of 1711 by Bishop John Sage, Scottish Episcopalian and Tory, the suitably mellifluous and romantic Victorian account by David Masson, and L. E. Kastner's two-volume edition of the *Poetical Works* of 1913. Since then, they have persevered.

What did he have to complain of? Among his papers is a document, entitled 'Memorials', which proves to be a catalogue of 'fatalities'. It lists falls from horses and down stairs. He is almost drowned at sea. One afternoon he 'voided a great gravel stone'. Colic and the stone were 'the pain of all pains'. Gout in the big toe of his left foot and in his right foot – an affliction which, as my own left foot was to attest, is apt to visit the 'forlorn castaway' he imagined himself to be. In 1625 'I suspected myself to have been poisoned.' In 1639 he 'escaped a fearful wandering in the night by the providence almighty going alone through moss and coalpits'. Twice he 'almost' broke his collar bone through the stumblings of those horses of his. The accidents he lists can be called historical, and they do not figure in his verse. And they are very far from being the sum of his ill luck.

Several of his documentary disasters are 'almosts', however, and he survived in one piece until 1649. His writings give the sense we sometimes have of the instability of complaint. Is the complainer, we may want to know, a seeker or inventor of mishaps, accident-prone, a hypochondriac, a malingerer? There have been many weepers, and the weeper has many names, many of them sceptical or impatient. Such questions perplexingly arise in relation to the best-known of Drummond's misfortunes: the death by fever of the woman he is thought to have been about to marry – a Miss Cunningham of Barns in Fife. This woman has in recent years been deemed to be Euphemia Cunningham, who died, some three months after Shakespeare did, in the summer of 1616.

His principal book of verse, the two-part *Poems*, an assembly of sonnets, madrigals, sextains and long 'songs', was published in the same year. David Masson was persuaded that the second part mourned the woman's death. But recent scholarship has undertaken to show that the 'funeral' poems contained there were written before she died, and has argued that such poems as Drummond's sonnets are impersonal rather than confessional. We should not make the romantic mistake of supposing that they express the poet's '*real* feelings'. We should not do as Masson did and call the second part of the *Poems* 'a Memorial of his Love and his Sorrow', while speaking of the first part in terms of 'a little history of love and its painful deliciousness'. The diminutive certainly does seem out of place.

Drummond's father and uncle bore office in the court of James VI, who was to flit to London when Drummond was eighteen. Declining the profession of law, Drummond settled at Hawthornden, with his books, his lute, his griefs, his self-pity. When he came to rebuild this hermitage, he inscribed on a wall the words: *Aedificavit Drummondus ut honesto otio quiesceret*. He had fashioned the Metaphysical conceit of a cottage castle for the studious, virtuous leisure of a patrician recluse – a vertiginous cottage castle which stands on a rock in whose entrails is a prehistoric cave dwelling, and which has a terrace that looks out over the all but touchable tops of very tall trees, down into a glen crowded with the sepulchral greens of their foliage and threaded by the River Esk, a matching colour, long poisoned by dyeworks. The place is both large and small, both astonishing and endearing. The annals and achievements of landscape as gesture and as décor, of the *paysage moralisé*, can exhibit few creations quite like Hawthornden, where Drummond drew his horizons towards him like bedclothes, so that he could be both on top of the world and well out of it.

> What sweet delight a quiet life affords,
> And what it is to be of bondage free,
> Far from the madding worldlings' hoarse discords,
> Sweet flowery place, I first did learn of thee.

In the pastoral seclusion inhabited by his sonnets Drummond played the part of Damon, with his absent or reluctant love, who eventually dies, and his friend Alexis, alias Sir William Alexander, poet and politician. Having translated the Psalms of David with King James, Alexander went on to be a coloniser, to become Viscount Canada, while Drummond stayed at home, forswearing courts and Nova Scotias. Alexis is asked to inscribe on his friend's grave the epitaph:

> Here Damon lies, whose songs did sometime grace
> The murmuring Esk, may roses shade the place.

Drummond, though, was not inflexibly reclusive. Kastner's edition copiously identifies him as a reader of other poets, as their companion, and as their imitator. This has had something of a deterrent effect, I think. His imitations can be seen as inroads on his solitude, and they can make him seem, as his woes can make him seem, weak. Here, perhaps, is an analogue to the frailty caught in his most celebrated line: 'A hyacinth I wisht me in her hand.' But they do not make him a thief. Poets do this, and Early Modern poets could take pride in it, pleasure in it, in the companionate renewals, reversals and ripostes, copies and captures, which were reckoned to have belonged to the making of poetry ever since the holy work began, ever since the beginning of their world. One of the lines I have been quoting is quoted – the recyclist recycled – in Gray's Elegy, where it appears as 'Far from the madding crowd's ignoble strife'; and a hundred years after Drummond's ailing *floruit*, and just before Gray's, Lady Mary Wortley Montagu paid tart attention to the familiar strain of lovelorn pastoral sorrow and turned it inside out. A grieving female was advised:

> All those dismal looks and fretting
> Cannot Damon's life restore.

In various capacities, moreover, Drummond was willing to desert his quiet corner of Albany, a poet's name for a region of what was later to be styled North Britain, and to take part in the tormented public life of his time. Not only did he assemble one of the most significant libraries of the Renaissance: he added to it histories and political tracts of his own. He served the Stuart cause, and in so doing became the advocate of a benevolent despotism. Not for him the democratically-accountable monarchy of George Buchanan's *De Iure Regni apud Scotos*: and yet the

Drummond who recognised the importance of toleration and the existence of a commonweal must count as a critic of the version of divine right expounded in King James's *Basilikon Doron*. Nevertheless, the totalitarian democracy, as he saw it, of a Presbyterian state was experienced as revolution, as a Caledonian Vespers, and as one of the darkest of his misfortunes. In earlier years he had contributed, as had John Donne, to the chorus of eager poems which mourned the death of Prince Henry, James's son: this was his first published poem, *Tears on the Death of Moeliades*. And when James returned to Scotland on a royal visit, the River Forth went over the top in Drummond's panegyric:

> Do I behold that worth, that man divine,
> This age's glory, by these banks of mine?

A similar welcome was extended to a Northern progress by Charles I.

Drummond's *Poems* of 1616 – the year before James's visit – had been preceded by an edition which appears to be made up of pre-publication proof sheets, and which has many of the poems on the death that coincides in the *Poems* with their green-eyed, golden-haired Auristella. This 'trial edition' has been conjecturally dated 1614. The description is used by Robert MacDonald, in the Introduction to his *William Drummond of Hawthornden: Poems and Prose* (1976), which speaks of 'real' feelings and claims that 'Drummond completed his "poems funerall" at least a year before Miss Cunningham's death' in 1616: what happens in the sonnets is 'conventional more than autobiographical', and 'most of Renaissance art' is like that. But if the death mourned in Part Two of the *Poems* does not refer to an actual death, Drummond's betrothed may none the less be present in the book as an attribute of the loved one of the protracted courtship which is described there, and which is shown as troubled by absences and refusals on her part. Could he have mourned the loved one's death – in conventional style and with recourse to translations from French, Italian and Spanish poetry – while his Miss Cunningham was still alive, while hoping to marry her and enduring the vicissitudes of a courtship? The usual vicissitudes of a courtship are one thing. The imagining of a death seems quite another.

And yet it is possible to think that Drummond may have acted in this way, and to think that the occasions of his life and the occasions of his verse belong to the one work of the imagination, to the closet of a man whose sonnets say that he must both 'write and love'; it is possible to think that they belong to a process in which what was to happen could be foreseen and foresuffered. As Keats was to say of Adam's dream, he awoke and found it truth. On one occasion, in Part One, he dreams of a lover's frustration or defeat:

> Me thought I set me by a cypress shade,
> And night and day the hyacinth there read.

The flower is an emblem of his grief, spelling out in its botanical aspect, as it was then taken to do, the letters AI – meaning 'Alas'. A few lines later the poem comes to an end:

> For what into my troubled brain was painted,
> I waking found that time and place presented.

This is to say that Miss Cunningham's death was predicted in the reveries of his youthful poems – reveries which were themselves predicted in the forlorn foreign poems, and in the forlorn ones of Philip Sidney, which instructed his sadness and enabled him to write poems which long found unfortunates to instruct, and which found a disastered Me, a bus ride from his hermitage, in Gilmerton, Edinburgh, where I sat in my closet with his hefty works, scanning the portraits of him, with their alternately bleak and lustrous round eyes and frilly moustache, plattered on ruffs and frilly collars. 'Framed for mishap', the 'orphan' author of his first poems knew that 'all beneath the Moon decays,' and expected his rough ride. In Drummond, one might feel, outset and outcome meet, design and accident meet. And one might also feel that the manner a poet assumes, the themes he takes, the translations he makes, are as autobiographical as any of the other memorials of his life. To say all this of Drummond is to represent him as in some sense a seeker of misfortune, married to one of the styles native to the conditioning of a Renaissance poet. But it is as well to add that the conventional Drummond was capable of telling an unidentified woman, in an undated letter, that a poem or poems by him were done for her. Her beauty and 'good parts' had made him pregnant.

In Fife, his Miss Cunningham was a neighbour of his friend and brother-in-law Scot of Scotstarvet. A local stream, the Ore, is mentioned in Part One of the *Poems*, and appears to have been embodied in the name Auristella, which also alludes to Sidney's Stella; Auristella is the poet's 'northern phoenix', to be found by the Ore. This might seem to allot a presence in the book to the betrothed. A passage from a Song in Part Two runs:

> Who would have thought to me
> The place where thou didst lie could grievous be?
> And that (dear body) long thee having sought
> (O me!) who would have thought?
> Thee once to find it should my soul confound,
> And give my heart than death a deeper wound?

Is this the imaginary woman of Renaissance art? Many readers might well feel that this must be the same woman who is evoked in relation to the doleful premonitory dream I have mentioned. It is dreamt by the banks of the Ore, and it belongs to a Song in Part One, where it concludes a visionary sequence in which three sisters bathe in the stream and are consigned to a diamantine fortress of chastity. Many readers might also feel that this woman could be seen as the commemoration of a particular person (and of a long courtship) – as the commemoration of a woman Drummond knew, and not just 'the idea of a woman'. The quoted words are those of Ben Jonson, who told Drummond that Donne had used them to explain that his poem in praise of the unknown Elizabeth Drury had been an idealisation. Donne's paragon has the qualities that Eliot was to praise in Donne. A thought to her was an experience. One might almost say that her body thought. Jonson thought the poem would have been better if it had been about the Virgin Mary.

94

In the first part of the book, one of Drummond's most beautiful sonnets foresuffers the beloved's death in cadences fit to accompany some stately dance; an exotic word-order, leaning into Latin, assists the performance. His sonnets are given to performing in this way – calling to mind a ceremony of melancholy music, paces and pauses. The same ceremony, and the same geography, occur in Sidney's sonnet 'With how sad steps, Oh Moon, thou climb'st the skies', whose 'heavenly place' could be felt to have predicted the 'lower place' of Drummond's sonnet, which begins:

> How many times night's silent queen her face
> Hath hid, how oft with stars in silver mask
> In Heaven's great hall she hath begun her task,
> And cheered the waking eye in lower place.

This is a poem about a woman's absence which could be read as a poem about a death. Nights and days will pass, but count them up as he may, it will be a long time before he sees her again, and 'her absence makes me die.' That closing statement, with its possible epigrammatic stress on the disastered self (as who should say, her death will be the death of *me*), may permit such a reading, and might suggest that the book as a whole could be read as a fiction of bereavement which unites Parts One and Two, and in which, to speak gruesomely, the real woman who may be thought to have contributed to it is finally buried alive. According to this fiction, the absence and indifference of the beloved are succeeded by the death from which they have at moments been barely distinguishable. Both parts of the book are full of intimations of mortality, and Drummond's own demise is spoken of, and at times desired. 'I long to kiss the image of my death': Part One glitters with such starry wishes.

It is difficult to be certain that the pre-writing of the funeral poems took place. It is also difficult to construct a rival account. With his defunctive tastes and adaptive skills (a third of his productions, it has been estimated, are translations and paraphrases, and the chief mourner among his sonnets, 'As in a dusky and tempestuous night', is a cento assembled from two sonnets by Tasso), Drummond could be thought to have been able to respond to Euphemia's death in preparing the 1616 volume for publication. But the time for this would surely have been very short, and it would be easier to entertain the possibility if the date for the trial edition, with so many of the death poems, had not been set, if only 'tentatively', at 1614.

Drummond's betrothed is called Euphemia Cunningham by MacDonald, in the course of his efforts to exclude her from the poems in which she had been seen – efforts which have depended on a laudatory sonnet of Drummond's dedicated to Euphemia (before being re-dedicated to a Countess of Perth) and dating her death. In the past, the betrothed had occasionally been called Mary, but not much can be made (by me) of the earlier name. It might lead one to ask if Euphemia could have had a sister – one of three Graces, as .t were – who predeceased her and who occasioned the funeral poems. What little information has survived concerning the family turns out, however, to suggest an only daughter, and the allegory of love imparted in Drummond's dream poem is unlikely, without corroboration, to appear more than piquant to those who attempt to decide between the view that Euphemia was the woman he was hoping to marry, at a time when he may also have been writing Petrarchan poems on the death of the beloved, and the traditional view that these are elegies on the death of a woman he knew.

The first view has its appeal for the temperament ascribed to myself in the present book, while the second seems rather more in keeping with my experience of the poems. Neither view requires one to believe in the absence of the betrothed from both parts of the 1616 volume. We are free to think that there was a young woman who lived in Fife, and that this woman's life, if not her death, entered the Arcadia of Drummond's imagination. So much for my researches into the identity of the blonde Dark Lady of his sonnets.

David Masson's version of Drummond's Arcadia was dewily adopted and adapted in my radio play, which dramatised a visit by the suitor to Fife and devised a would-be witty love scene in a boat on the Forth. These scenes featured a Scottishly malapert betrothed – a Euphemia, or Effie, who was known to me then as Mary. She joins her lover in pastoral badinage, and Drummond was handed some verse of my own with which to extemporise:

> Old Triton here has just caught sight
> Of sable-stoled and shady Night
> Come hand in hand with Hesperus
> From a crimson West to worry us.

In the years that followed Miss Cunningham's death, while in his thirties, Drummond had a mistress, who is absent both from Masson's biography and from my play. Then, in his mid-forties, he married. He had three children by the mistress, nine by the wife. These experiences go unfictionalised, and indeed unmentioned, in his poems. His poetry may for the most part be said to have housed the orphan Drummond of the love poems and the exalted and rhapsodic Christian Platonist; his writings make use of a Medieval cosmology while acknowledging the Copernican iconoclasm – so that an Earth which has been held to move still enjoys its Heavens above. But the solemn, sweet and unfortunate Drummond is not the only poet to be seen in his collected works. There are others.

Among them is the funny and dirty misogynistic Drummond whom we discover when we turn to the occasional and satirical verse which has been attributed to him. This could perhaps register as evidence of an abrasive narcissism, among readers who might also be willing to believe that the proleptic death inflicted on a fiancée became the injury to women inflicted in the poems of his *dubia* or apocrypha. My radio play cites Coleridge's opinion that Drummond suffered from the deficient sense of humour 'characteristic of a Scotchman', who 'has no notion of a jest, unless you tell him – *This is a joke!* still less of that shade of feeling, the half-and-half'. Drummond did make jokes, however, and he certainly made jests, and one or two of his jokes are funny. Rather more of them are dirty.

Coleridge's opinion posits an un-English Drummond, and can be contrasted with an opinion of the editors of the *Oxford Book of Scottish Verse* (1966), from which Drummond was virtually excluded on the grounds that he belongs to an English literary tradition. Will this man's troubles never end? Alistair Fowler's *New Oxford Book of Seventeenth-Century Verse* made amends in 1991 by offering a generous and judicious selection of twenty-seven items. 'And of course there is always Drummond,' writes C. S. Lewis in *English Literature in the Sixteenth Century*. 'But Drummond himself, when all's said, is a Scotchman only "out of school".' Meaning, presumably, only when he isn't writing. Lewis is referring, a little wearily, to a spell of drought in Scottish literature, with Drummond too English to count as relief.

The sentence is preceded by an allusion to another Scotchman, Mark Alexander Boyd, who died in 1601. Boyd is the author, in Scots, of just the one poem, the rest of his verse being in Latin, and I remember the day when Hector MacIver chalked up this Scots poem on the blackboard. The power of the victim is displayed there. Leaping about the countryside like the outcast king of Medieval Irish literature, weakness runs wild, speaking its frenzy in masterful verse, in which a Reformation severity and a Renaissance single speaker have been observed. Drummond's sonnets on a subjection to sexual love, while commemorative of other poets' work, can be thought both commemorative and personal: but none of them touches the reader as this sonnet does with the sense of a living individual – and of a no less literary individual who is nevertheless nothing of an imitator. What Hector wrote on the board – on another day it carried MacDiarmid's 'The Bonnie Broukit Bairn', which has in it, as the Boyd has, both Venus and a child – was this:

> Fra bank to bank, fra wood to wood I rin,
>> Ourhailit with my feeble fantasie;
>> Like til a leaf that fallis from a tree,
> Or til a reed ourblawin with the win'.
> Twa gods guides me; the ane of them is blin',
>> Yea and a bairn brocht up in vanitie;
>> The next a wife ingenrit of the sea,
> And lichter nor a dauphin with her fin.

Unhappy is the man for evermair
   That tills the sand and sawis in the air;
   But twice unhappier is he, I lairn,
That feedis in his hairt a mad desire,
And follows on a woman throw the fire,
   Led by a blind and teachit by a bairn.

The least funny of Drummond's jokes consists of a poem in which he addresses a woman whom he had once, he says, 'done wrong' and who has since given herself to all and sundry, kinsmen included. She is urged to try her children's tutor,

                    who well can
Teach any woman to decline to man,
That will himself a diphthong turn with you.

She is subjected to robustly versified abuse (not lost on Alistair Fowler), of a kind both highly educated and profane. She is like Sir Francis Drake's boat, which, having 'sailed all seas', is now waterlogged; her breasts are 'like sodden haggises'. The poem ends with the polar opposite of the Petrarchan sonneteer of 1616:

Let me alone, and force me not to enter.
If Hell be into earth it's in your centre.

Drummond is a poet of mixed feelings, of compacted sweets and sours: such a poet might well reveal a scabrous or spiteful counterpart – a Rochester shadow-self – in relation to the wretchedness exhibited by the Damon of the sonnets, though it's also true that the present poem has its own note of complaint ('let me alone' – this from someone who ought to have been asked to let the woman alone). Such thoughts might lead one to a Drummond and Hyde, to discover within the victim an aggressor, worst enemy of the weakling who wanted to be held in some woman's hand.

Hawthornden duality embodied, in Classical style, a contemplation of opposites, and there's a sonnet on the subject at the start of Part One.

Fair is my yoke, though grievous be my pains,
Sweet are my wounds, although they deeply smart,
My bit is gold, though shortened be the reins,
My bondage brave, though I may not depart:
Although I burn, the fire which doth impart
Those flames so sweet reviving force contains
That (like Arabia's bird) my wasted heart,
Made quick by death, more lively still remains.
I joy, though oft my waking eyes spend tears,
I never want delight, even when I groan,
Best companied when most I am alone,
A heaven of hopes I have midst hells of fears:
    Thus every way contentment strange I find,
    But most in her rare beauty, my rare mind.

O rare William Drummond. Elsewhere he says his mind is 'sick'. Here he is both sick and well. The poem describes the paradoxical state of the lover in whose experience opposites meet. It is a state which resembles that known to the alchemical tradition – where the world was a concoction of the four elements and the four humours – as a 'strange compound'. It suggests that the lover's opposites ensure a convivial solitude: 'Best companied when most I am alone'. This rehearses the Latin commonplace *Numquam minus solum quam cum solus*, which, obtained by Cicero from Scipio Africanus, became popular in Britain, among shunners of popularity and adepts of duality, during the later eighteenth century and the Romantic period. The poem shows a dependence on the ancient world and a presentiment of the Romantic one. Drummond is easily felt to have been an ur-Romantic; this indeed is the life that Masson chose to write.

It is possible to relate this highly symptomatic poem to the states described in the nineteenth-century literature of duality, and to think of Drummond as a strange compound of the wretched lover, the holy thinker, the prince's friend, the ill-conditioned man about court. The sad words used in this poem and in other such poems by him – 'orphan', 'forlorn' and the

like – may be said to contain anticipations of later modes of
feeling. The same can be said of his Moon-watching and of
other predilections of his. The prophecies here are of the self-
fulfilling sort – so far as he may be thought to have belonged to
a company of Early Modern miserables whose words have
remained influential ever since. His 'black map of all my woe'
was due to be succeeded by the frets, feats and virtuosity of a
later sonneteer, Dylan Thomas, with his no less distressful 'map
of love'. There may also be those who might claim, as did my
seldom unforthcoming radio play, that in his worries about mob
rule he 'foresuffered' the 'modern era'.

Drummond believed that the complex or compounded human
being inhabited a complex world in which God's order embraced
an infinite diversity. In the prose remonstrance 'Irene', a plea for
amity and peace composed at the time of the National Covenant
in 1638, when Charles I and the Presbyterian Scots were at a
point of crisis over prelacy, he drew on the language of the
astronomer and the alchemist, or spagyrick, to form a more than
purely decorative argument for political toleration. He was in
favour of that, while especially disposed to tolerate the absolut-
ism of such rulers as the Stuart kings, provided they exercised
restraint and showed consideration. On behalf of the weak man
evident in his poems, he intercedes with the strong man – the
man divine – of hereditary right. The good are weak, he writes
in his meditation 'A Cypress Grove' (1623). They are 'but
forlorn castaways', while 'the most wicked are lords and gods of
this earth' – though in the years to come he would think of the
Stuart dynasty, in its evil hour, as so many forlorn castaways. At
all events, alchemical multiplicity authorised a policy of live and
let live, and 'Irene' has a passage on the subject, which says
(contrary, *if I may make a Scottish joke*, to my first impressions of
the Irish) that no two faces are the same, and goes on to say that
we should be kind to others.

> Yea, not only this Universe in general, but there is no
> creature in it, not a body, not a simple, that is not composed
> and existing with some diversity. Gems, gold, the minerals,

the elements exist not pure: the planets have a motion contrary to the first movable: yet is there a perfect harmony in all this great frame and a discording concord maketh all the parcels of it delightful. Of the diversity and variety which is in this world ariseth that beauty so wonderful and amazing to our eyes. In architecture diversity doth not destroy uniformity: the limbs of a noble fabric may be correspondent enough, though they be various. We find not two persons of one and the same shape, figure and lineaments of the face, less of the same conditions, qualities, humours, though they be of the self-same parents, and why do we seek to find men all of one thought and one opinion in formalities and matters disputable? Or, if they shall be found dissonant and disagreeing from the vulgarly received opinions, or errors, why should we by our fancy and law of power banish, proscribe, design or expose them to slaughter?

Earlier in Drummond's life there appeared in Albany a foreign body in the massive person of Ben Jonson, who, in 1618, trudged north for four hundred miles in pursuit of his ancestors and of literary material that might please King James. Two weeks of that Christmas season were spent at Hawthornden, and passages of the talk that ensued were recorded by the host. These conversations are an early masterpiece of informal criticism and authorial display. There was a time when it was said that Drummond had betrayed his guest, which was also a time when Coleridge said that Drummond had been betrayed by his Scotchman's lack of humour: 'These notes of Drummond ought never to have been published. They are more disgraceful to himself than to Jonson. It would be easy to conjecture Jonson's comments on them – how grossly he had been misunderstood, and what he had said in jest (as of Hippocrates) interpreted in earnest.' These may be thought chauvinistic reactions, and intensely ungrateful ones. The notes were published in full in 1833, having appeared in digest form many years before.

I fell on this visit for my feature programme, quoting from Drummond's notes and inventing colourful stuff for Jonson to declaim. The scenes in question were introduced by some lines from Walter Scott's dirge for the lovely Rosabelle, whelmed in the waters of Drummond's Hellespont, the Firth of Forth:

> O'er Roslin all that dreary night,
>   A wondrous blaze was seen to gleam;
> 'Twas broader than the watch-fire's light,
>   And redder than the bright moonbeam.
>
> It glared on Roslin's castled rock,
>   It ruddied all the copse-wood glen;
> 'Twas seen from Dryden's groves of oak,
>   And seen from cavern'd Hawthornden.

What, in the context of the radio play, was this fire? It was, said the script, 'the fine frenzy of a poet. Ben Jonson's wondrous blaze was painting the glen red.' A Grand Cham of London letters had come to visit Scotland, and to delight and offend its notables, just as another was to do, in the person of Jonson's namesake Samuel. A sterling duo. And there was to be another such visitor. At about the time the play was being written, Dylan Thomas arrived among the Edinburgh literati. At one point he asked Robert Taubman, just like that, how he 'made his money'. In most of Edinburgh then, you did not ask such questions.

According to Bishop Sage, Drummond was not a drinker: he would share a bottle only *ad hilaritatem*. According to Drummond, Jonson

> is a great lover and praiser of himself; a contemner and scorner of others; given rather to lose a friend than a jest; jealous of every word and action of those about him (especially after drink, which is one of the elements in which he liveth); a dissembler of ill parts which reign in him, a bragger of some good that he wanteth; thinking nothing well but what either he himself or some of his friends and countrymen hath said or done: he is passionately kind and angry; careless either to gain or keep; vindicative, but, if he be well answered, at himself. For any religion, as

being versed in both. Interpreteth best sayings and deeds often to the worst. Oppressed with phantasy, which hath ever mastered his reason, a general disease in many poets. His inventions are smooth and easy; but above all he excelleth in a translation.

Literary talk runs true to type throughout these conversations – in all its jealousy and boasting, its 'how much did I get for it', its technical points, its other people's mistakes, its 'others must fail'. Jonson evidently felt the disinhibition of the visiting writer. He beat Marston up 'and took his pistol from him', Drummond learned. The self-serving violent directness of the transcribed opinions of contemporary writers is a rich vein. Shakespeare 'wanted art', said Jonson, who also conveyed that he didn't know his geography. Donne, 'for not keeping of accent, deserved hanging' – for not following the beat, the metrical stress; and 'from not being understood, would perish'. 'The King said Sir P. Sidney was no poet,' reported Jonson, adding that Sidney's face – that pool in which Jonson's host had so often seen his own – was 'spoiled with pimples'.

What did he think of Drummond? My play has Jonson discoursing on Scotland: 'weird Cisalpine domain that it is, where the monsters and the men, geographers relate, are double-tongued and two-faced. And where their heads grow underneath their arms, like bagpipes and like Tudor ghosts.' This passage predicts the interest I was to take in literary duality: but neither in the play nor in Jonson's recorded opinion of his host is there any inkling of a double Drummond. 'He said to me that I was too good and simple, and that oft a man's modesty made a fool of his wit.' This chimes with a probably fanciful story that used to be told of Drummond: it has him putting his shy head round the door of a room in London – to be greeted as 'Bo-Peep' by a gathering of poets, hungry for pastoral, which included Ben Jonson.

Jonson's 'censure of my verses was that they were all good, especially my Epitaph of the Prince, save that they smelled too much of the Schools, and were not after the fancy of the time.'

The Schools, presumably, were those of the Continent – the Petrarchans, the Pléiade. For a clue to 'the fancy of the time' it is worth turning to a letter of Drummond's, addressed several years later to the third of this chapter's Johnsons – the Scotsman Arthur Johnston, Charles I's physician and a noted Latin poet. The letter treats of English monsters.

This may have been the first occasion on which the term 'metaphysical' was applied to the poetry which has since been called by that name – a name which until quite recently was conventionally credited to Dryden and to Samuel Johnson. Ben Jonson would have felt that the fancy of the time lay with, or encompassed, himself and the Metaphysicals, to whose poetry his own bore certain resemblances. He censured Sidney and Donne for offences against decorum; he himself was a Classical stickler, and a scanner. But his verse owned a speaking voice, showed something of Donne's conscious 'harshness', was vigorous rather than sonorous, and (*pace* Drummond) was at least as reasonable as it was fantastical. Jonson told his host (while also telling him different at other times) that 'verses stood by sense without either colours or accent.' Drummond admired Donne's 'Anacreontic' lyricism, while thinking it a low flyer in the skies of literature. He stood by colours and accent and ornament, and could sometimes be said to lack sense. But there was a 'sense of the writer' which, as a reader of poetry, he wanted to reach, and which he felt confident of sharing with the famous poets of the past. Fine-spinning, abstraction and innovation were alien to poetry – which was not a becoming but an already there. His sonnets were a saraband of silver and gold in which precedent was respected and fulfilled, and the fashionable alternative of the poetry to which Jonson's bore resemblances was monstrous.

His guest may, in other words, have appeared to him to be leagued with a breed of monsters who had broken with the past, and he complains about them in his letter to Arthur Johnston. Of the eminence and long duration of 'poesy' he writes:

> There is not anything endureth longer: Homer's Troy hath
> outlived many republics, and both the Roman and Grecian

monarchies. She subsisteth by herself, and after one demeanour and countenance her beauty appeareth to all ages. In vain have some men of late (transformers of everything) consulted upon her reformation, and endeavoured to abstract her to metaphysical ideas, and scholastical quiddities, denuding her of her own habits and those ornaments with which she hath amused the world some thousand years. Poesy is not a thing which is yet in the finding and search, or which may be otherwise found out, being already condescended upon by all nations, and as it were established *iure gentium*, amongst Greeks, Romans, Italians, French, Spaniards. Neither do I think that a good piece of poesy which Homer, Virgil, Ovid, Petrarch, Bartas, Ronsard, Boscan, Garlicasso (if they were alive, and had that language) could not understand, and reach the sense of the writer. Suppose these men could find out some other new idea like poesy, it should be held as if Nature should bring forth some new animal, neither man, horse, lion, dog, but which had some members of all, if they had been proportionably and by right symmetry set together. What is not like the ancients and conform to those rules which hath been agreed unto by all times may (indeed) be something like unto poesy, but it is no more poesy than a monster is a man. Monsters breed admiration at the first, but have ever some strange loathsomeness in them at last. I deny not but a mulet is more profitable than some horses, yet it is neither horse nor ass, and yet it is but a mulet. There is a tale told of a poor miserable fellow accused of bestiality, and he at his arraignment confessed that it was not out of any evil intention he had done it, but only to procreate a monster with which (having nothing to sustain his life) he might win his bread, going about the country. For the like cause it may be thought these men found out their new poesy differing from the matters, manners, rules of former ages: either they did not see the way of poesy or were afraid to enter it.

The complaint enabled him to tell what looks like a Scottish joke, which has what most of his jokes can hardly claim – humour, and a touch of human sympathy. The poor fellows who appear, one way and another, in his writings could be said to have something of a rival in the man who defended himself against a charge of bestiality by saying that there had been no wicked thought of pleasure – there had only been starvation, and a plan to beget a monster and zoo it round the shires for gain.

The alternative Drummond of his scabrous or satiric writings may or may not have been made known to his guest, and there is a sequence of posthumously published poems, about the five senses of his sovereign, which has been attributed to him and which Jonson might have enjoyed. His sovereign is the divine man whose coming causes the River Forth to overflow, in a very different poem of Drummond's. These poems are far from panegyrical: the borrower from Continental poets turns xenophobe and the alternative Drummond presents an alternative James, a ruler threatened by his homosexual infatuations.

> Next I crave
> Thou wilt be pleased, great God, to save
> My sovereign from a Ganymede,
> Whose whorish breath hath power to lead
> His excellence which way it list;
> O let such lips be never kissed
> From a breath so far excelling;
> Bless my sovereign and his smelling.

If there is a joke here, it may be seen as another Scottish one, which cries faugh to scents and cissies.

The story of excellent King James's five endangered senses and two faces would not look out of place in the register of Drummond's inconsistencies. It was inconsistent, too, of this peacemonger to turn his hand, in mid-life – as if in emulation of the neighbouring laird of Merchiston, John Napier, to whom we are indebted for both logarithms and the tank – to the patenting of engines of destruction, including a supergun and a battleship; and there was a device for shipboard desalination. His military inventions were awarded centipede Greek names;

the vulgar were allowed to call one of them, for short, The Elephant, and another Leviathan.

This was a time when new weapons were especially welcome. His final years were oppressed by the Civil War, and by debt, for which his investments in research and development must have been partly to blame. The recluse who took part in politics was given a letter of protection by Montrose in the course of Montrose's Northern exploits on behalf of Charles I, and thanked for his 'constant loyalty towards His Sacred Majesty'. This letter of 1646 speaks of Drummond's 'so much personal deserving'. In 1649 the King was beheaded, and Drummond died soon after. In the prose piece 'Irene' of 1638 he had written:

> The climacteric and period of the monarchical governments of Europe is not yet come, and when, or if ever, it shall come, ye who are Nobles will perish with it: for the commons, then all Princes, will not suffer in their statutes, edicts, ordinances any longer I, but We. In distribution and parting of honours, offices, riches, lands, they will proceed after an arithmetical proportion, and not a geometrical: towns will close their gates upon you, and ye may some day expect a Sicilian evensong.

It must have seemed to him in his last days that that time had come.

I thought when I was eighteen that Drummond's sonnets were beautiful, and I still think them beautiful. They are an extraordinary music. I hope that they can still be heard as such by those with an ear for verse, and I would be sorry to find that their cadences had been silenced by the talk of nationality and convention to which his work has been subjected. I knew when I was young that his complaints were grounded in translation and in imitation: but I also believed, as I still do, that the complaints are none the less his, and in later times I came to see in them an imagined pre-emption, a form of magical insurance against misfortune, a recital of worst cases, a hypothesis kissing-close to its fulfilment. Some part of this programme, I came to feel, could be attributed to myself – both to Drummond's adolescent reader and to his successors, holding on to their legends and adventures, and to their sad stories. I had been attracted by him, and I had also been warned.

I passed over the misogynist invectives, the priapic madrigals, when I was young, and had no notion of that play of contraries in his life and work which offers the paradox of a hyacinthine achiever and aggressor (his eirenic politics are not free from aggression). Like many another unfortunate, he was both active and productive. His woefulness is both weak and strong. Strong not least in its adherence to a pre-emptive and exploitative code of weakness. Weak, detractors might add, in its disclosure of the supine fellow who never stopped complaining, and who aspired to achieve, while arranging to appropriate,

> Works heavenly wise in sweet harmonious lays,
> Which sprites divine unto the world set forth.

His contradictions are evident in the conventions he obeyed and the imitations he pursued. Here are writings which reproduce the conventions, and in so doing reproduce the contradictions, of the past, writings which have much to show, for instance, of the bipart horror and adoration of women associated with the Courtly Love tradition. Here, too, is a man who has been blamed both for being a Scotsman and for being an Englishman, a man who was both, and who became both in responding to the fictions and conventions which create perceptions of national identity, to the precedents which had already begun to create the species Anglo-Scot.

CHAPTER SEVEN

The Nether Fields

With the exception of the story which supplies this chapter with a title, I paid virtually no attention to the Army till the Army paid attention to me, sending a writ and summoning me to Aldershot. Having some months before completed the story, in which I am much the worse for enemy action, I joined like a lamb.

At school – where I'd ended up as a poet and an editor, and as a prefect – I'd been rather more in my element than I realised at the time. At home, budgets had been tight, but there had never been any danger of going to the wall. I'd never felt deprived or lower-class. My experiences at school had been partly responsible for that, and they had made me, in a distraught sort of way, complacent. The kindness shown me by relatives and friends was sometimes to make me feel – while capable of feeling and certainly of saying the opposite – that all was well. All is never well.

I thought of National Service as a pause between school and university, as a kind of seventh form. The two years would be spent in the languorous attitudes of a pastoral poet, mooning by a Nissen hut with a book in my hand. This is what the verse of Alun Lewis and Sidney Keyes and many a *Penguin New Writing* had led me to expect of the Forces. It would be Woodbines, Woodbines all the way, and short stories, and yielding girls. Soldiers were sensitive and solitary. They were like Denton Welch. Privates enjoyed private lives of rare quality.

My own short story, 'The Nether Fields', which more or less went about with me, attached to my person, and which was later to see the light of publication in Cambridge, expressed this notion of the soldier as poet and loiterer. Loitering even unto death, my wounded man contemplates the indifferent behaviour of a fair-haired boy, who looks like the retrospect of a former self. So there are two me's to the tale, as I have suggested. I was told that the situation resembles the one to be found at the close of Thomas Mann's *Death in Venice*, which I had yet to read. The resemblance, gratifying though it was to be told of it, is not such as to encourage thoughts of a thematic congruence, and can scarcely be taken to indicate the presence at the heart of the story of homosexual longings, whether deathly or lively, sick or sound. The story is charged with adolescent narcissism. I was adoring my own youth in a military mirror which had precious little to do with the realities of military life.

The story opens with these words:

> I was wounded on the Alsace frontier during the war. One October night I was returning on my own from a raid, and was trying to find my unit again. The range of the shot was so close that I seemed to have been sniped at by my shadow; it was as if an instant's sun had bounded out of the slope into my face. I thought as I fell that it might have been one of my own platoon in mistake.

I am a member of a platoon here, but I am necessarily on my own; and despite my mortal wound, I have the leisure for a fanciful survey of the surrounding wood.

> On either side of me, the darkness of the wood presented a gentle, faded surface, like that of a tapestry, on which the trunks, branches and leaves were carefully embroidered. One might have expected a ghostly Tudor woman in a brocaded gown to stiffen beneath some tree, with the hanging shapes at her feet of a pack of hounds and a falcon sitting tidily on her glove. As I stared, taking my bearings, the figures in the texture took on the definition of a developed photograph looming through the negative; my perspectives, my depths emerged, and Gloriana became a tree.

There's a group of shattered farmhouses on my right, and on my left a country road. I make it to the barn and fall asleep on a bale of hay.

I come to, and find myself accommodated in this barn, with

its two carts, its tower of baskets and string of onions (France was onions for the youth who remembered the Onion or Ingan Johnnies who went about the countryside before the war), its old-gold hay and black shadows. 'Everything appeared deep and rich and removed from what was outside, where two fields away the road was' and where my platoon might show up. 'I felt secure, satisfied somehow, and then, my gaze happening on the door, I saw a boy standing there quietly with his hands by his side.' This is a very detached sort of boy, and there is a language problem – I have trouble following his French. A long sequence of questions and answers then unfolds, in which I try, not very availingly, to get the boy to go for help.

> I felt like Socrates, talking his life away on a pallet bed, dulled from the waist down by the mounting hemlock. My silent disciple, he did not move, being woven into the background of the barn. His fair hair was long, his eyes grey, his nose aquiline. In contrast with the softness and lightness of his body, the look in his eyes was sometimes heavy. While he was not good-looking, his features had the delicate beauty common to children of that age.

I fly into a rage of frustration, and the boy abruptly leaves, leaves me to muse on an agonising affinity, and to address the matters of friendship and communion which Robert Taubman and I had been in the habit of discussing. I thought about

> my frantic eagerness to come to some kind of terms with this second person. My energies had been directed, not towards the boy as he was, but probably more towards my own idea of him, ever since his slender presence had changed the atmosphere of my den. And I could not tell whether that idea was quite illusory or not. I only knew that I had tried to reach and secure this presence, insulated as it was, on my own behalf, and to unite it with myself.

After that, I lose consciousness again, while retaining my capacity for the familiar Classical allusion.

In my dreams, which were big and vivid, my old anger revived, so that I found myself attacking the boy with my two hands to choke him. I stretched him like a tiny Ixion round the rim of one of the cart wheels, till the muscles jumped in his calves. Next I saw him ferrying a company of the dead back over the nether river of my fields towards me as I lay waiting – and they had the faces of men who were soldiers with me, but whom no one had killed so far. In an uproar they proceeded many abreast through the hall of the barn, having come to help me not to die: but for all their vigour, they gave the impression only of marking time. March as hard as they could, none reached my scarlet bed. None reached me, till I opened my eyes to meet those of the boy as he stooped above the hay.

The boy has returned without prospect of help, but with a hurricane lamp and a picture of the Madonna, fetched, it seems, from his ruined farmhouse. He perches the lamp by the cart wheel on which he has just been racked, and props his Madonna against a bale of hay. Light that lamp, the writer may have felt, and there would be a rosy manger scene in the manner of Georges de La Tour. But the lamp goes unlit. 'I gave up deliberating whether in fact he bore in mind what I had said.' But I go on pondering the struggles, imperfections and partial successes of friendship. 'I could not reconcile the sympathy I felt for him with what he might feel for me. I might be a mere deathbed to him.'

With my back raised slightly, my leg so planted as to be free from strain, and the boy on his feet with his hands clasped, all I could do was talk and think, like a head hewed from a trunk of immovable stone. My torn tunic with its shoulder flash and the lance-corporal's stripes were by me as if they belonged to somebody else. A khaki swab canopied the wound, from which the blood still drained, welling up gently, like tears.

The war is somewhere else, the gunfire fainter. The night is clear and the white dawn is beginning. There's some talk between us about where I am to be buried, perhaps behind the henhouses, perhaps in 'the proper graveyard, among the other dead'; and then I catch sight of my platoon, groping their way towards their bren-carrier, pushing on, I suppose, to the arterial road a few miles away, 'for my own road was only a lane'. The boy tells me what I am watching. 'It's the soldiers,' he says. His posture is like that of the exemplary boy in George Moore's *Confessions*, whose 'broad fair breast' and 'head thrown back' I would not have forgotten.

With his lips parted in thought, his whole body seemed to be thrusting upwards from the ground, as a plant does. His legs were struck and tensed, then out of the waist came the breast and shoulders, like a flower in the bud opening from its series of green jackets, or as my fountain of pain grew tall out of its source.

I shuddered, but I could not stir any further; it was as if a foothill tried to edge away from a mountain chain. A weariness that gave a strange great pain made me want to burst into talk, and I could scarcely silence myself. The blood had stopped leaving me, the towering weariness arose, I was a pair of eyes in a cliff.

Above the level of the hedges, the men continued passing to the main road, reminding me of the ducks, gliding by in stately rows, like Queen Victorias, that I had shot at in fairgrounds. Now the range was two green fields, with a morning mist for backcloth. Time passed. The men and the night were going graciously from the coming dawn.

My heart was forced overwhelmingly by an access of vast, pointless excitement. My temples were covered in sweat and my stiffened limbs were trembling. The murderous elation finished and left me quiet again.

The boy stood with his back to me, gazing at the sun as it grew out of the horizon. His arm was tinged with its light. I remembered every contact of his slim spirit, which no one could annexe.

The same emotion seized me, and slackened again. The contours of the land inside my doorway were white and shining in the dawn, as they would be with snow in the winter that would soon be here. I imagined that winter, rising as swiftly as this day's sun to be shed on the countryside and the barn. And, out of reach, the soldiers still went slowly through the wintry dawn.

Then, as I watched, my weariness was a towering pain, which rose irresistibly into that highest instant when, remembering how the dawn would change my woods, seeing the boy stand in the doorway in the sun, and across the fields and almost at the road, I died.

So that was my story, or the gist of it. There I was at eighteen, minded to practise dying, the art of it. 'The Nether Fields' was the *pas de deux* of myself, a disaster dance of the two me's, performing its awkward allegory of friendship, of friendship's never-ending negotiations and incomprehensions, at an age when people have the heart to think in such terms. Somewhere in the dreamwork of the story, I shouldn't wonder, were my discursive and affectionate relations with the older man. On another level, it was the observation of a past self, with the death of that self displaced – turned into the death of the observer. That observer is now a good deal further from me than his past self was from him. His past self was indeed breathing down his neck, inviting the violence of the rite of passage which is also present in the story. Dug from the pit of my adolescence, the story is bound to seem, to many readers, distinctly unwell: a pretentious sixth-form caper that should have been left to rot. But this Lazarus meant quite as much to me at the time as did anything that happened during my two years of Army life, for which it can hardly have served to steel my mind.

The Royal Engineers of Farnborough proved a very different element from the Royal High School of Edinburgh, and my experiences in basic training were a vile come-down or coming-to for the literary scholarship boy. It was immediately clear that loitering – known to the Army as skiving – was a practice which was especially condemned. After that delusive pastoral prelude, my National Service became burlesque – a comedy in two acts, interlarded with the odd scene of horror and despair. School was meritocratic: scholars and athletes were promoted and awarded badges. An authoritarian system, just as the Army was: but it appeared that the Army was something other than meritocratic, or at any rate that authority rested on a highly specialised conception of merit. You were likely to be made a second lieutenant if you had been to a public school, and could stand up to the rigours of an Officers' Training School, for which public schools were a fitting preparation. You were unlikely, by and large, to be exposed to these rigours if you had not been to a public school, and if you spoke with a regional accent.

As soon as I entered my first Hampshire hut, I noticed that there were two types of inmate, and it didn't need exhaustive research to establish which was earmarked for abrupt and exalted promotion. As a working-class scholarship boy on his way to a university, I seemed to hover between the two. I became friendly with another Scotsman, but a Scotsman who had been to a Scottish public school, and who was no Jock and didn't sound like one. When he left to win his spurs, I thought I wouldn't see him again. But I did.

On arriving at Farnborough, we discovered we had fallen through a hole and landed in the eighteenth century. Even in an unglamorous regiment like the Sappers, an Army unit behaved like an appendage of the landed interest and its suburban simulations: the game we were playing was gentry-and-mob, with touches of knights-and-serfs. The class arrangements of modern Britain had been collapsed into a simple dualism. There were two of everything: officers and other ranks, mess and cookhouse, cheesecutter and beret. It appeared that the Army had yet to develop a middle class. During the war, I gathered, this dualism had to some extent been dismantled, in order that we might win; merit, together with a measure of solidarity, had been given a chance. But the two tiers had returned. The subaltern from Oundle and his soldier-servant – Robin and Batman – loomed large over Hampshire. I can now see that there was method, of a kind, in this madness, and that merit has its madness too. But it looked at the time as if the Army had found a damned good way of restricting the supply of competent leaders.

I'd thought the Army would be sweet and secluded. Before long Robin was sneering at me as I stood to attention in front of him, having made one of the Army's actual or notional mistakes: 'You know what thought did.' Again, during the war, the military code of bullying and threats and sneers had been relaxed – for efficiency's sake and out of respect for what was going on. Now it was back. Perhaps it had been revived, in exaggerated form, in order to deal with the nothing-much-to-do National Service influx.

The initial humiliations seemed to be contrived to break you and toughen you simultaneously, and the more impressionable members of each intake, sitting in their 'spiders' or huts, were to sink at once into various states of misery and hostility. In the troopships at Harwich the tannoy used to request the officers to stay on shore while the other ranks were 'being loaded', like a netful of gorillas or a deck of refrigerated whalemeat. One corporal used to work himself up into cleverly paced and modulated fits of Hitlerian rage every time he took charge of a squad. One backward boy was made to double round the square until he dropped. Deaths were rumoured. It must have been difficult for the Regular Army to cope with the conscript swarms of the Fifties, but there was no sense in trying quite so hard to turn them into enemies. Many working-class boys had remained, until then, remarkably innocent of what it was to be treated like dirt, having at least been spared the boarding-school regime which was thought to have made officer material of the others. Now we knew.

Night fell as I entered a new camp. I'd been to the Q Stores to draw my kit, and had stumbled out into the dusk carrying my possessions in my arms. Presently they toppled over onto the wet road: blankets, denims, beret, cap-badge, shoulder flashes, belt, blanco. My 'housewife' burst open and its needle, thread and buttons flew off into the dark and took a long time to retrieve. This was a lot better than being shot in the groin, but for a moment there I seemed to lose all hope. After a while I collected my belongings and went on to the 'spider' where my mates were lying on their beds, reading comics, listening to the pop song 'Truly, truly fair' on the radio, and displaying and discussing their erections. Privates, it seemed, led very public lives.

I grew to be obsessed, as you had to, with the business of tending my boots and uniform and rifle. The battledress we wore was unsightly, uncomfortable and inconvenient, but you had to generate a fetishist's awareness of its textures and tortures. Those gaiters. The Army's idea of cleaning things was to make them dirty – if possible, to smear them with black lead. I became a connoisseur of salutes, and I'll never forget one corporal's performance in that area. His salute started as a foppish grovel and flowered into a soaring semaphoric orchid or flamingo: a show of exotic servility which sent up the officer and was clearly prejudicial to good order and military discipline, but which was quite unchargeable as such: a masterpiece of false ceremony, richly deserved.

I learnt some of the tricks of the trade, but I wasn't a success even as a skiver, and there were catastrophes. I was sent to a mill where octogenarian millers were hefting bags of flour: when one old man placed a bag on my narrow shoulders, I melted – ill-named – to the floor. I scored nothing out of twenty in an intelligence test in which you assembled the parts of a bicycle pump: for this I was placed among the clerks for what was left of my basic training. A psychiatrist talked to me with a displeased indifference which was impressive even by the exacting standards of his profession, and when I pried into my secret personal documents, handed to me under seal when I was posted abroad, I found that I wasn't considered to be leadership material.

And so to Act Two – in which I escape to Germany and spend the remainder of my National Service there. The British Forces Network radio station in Hamburg was a bizarre posting, and a deliverance. My feature programme on Drummond had helped to deliver me; and I'd also done some broadcasting after being called up. Officers who had been sneering and jeering the day before would tiptoe up behind you as you stood to attention on parade and pass on in whispers telephone messages from producers. Robin respected the BBC.

BFN was a queer place in more ways than one, but it did a fair job. It was a kind of local radio station, in advance of what there is now in that line – serving the British Army of the Rhine in a fashion that used at one time to be called participatory: soldiers, wives, Church Army canteen manageresses, would come to the microphone. On Sunday mornings *Two-Way Family Favourites*, a record-request programme, was broadcast jointly with the BBC in London. BFN's military broadcasters were divided into conscripts and regulars; there were civilians on secondment; there was an admin group of earthy soldiers who were sceptical of all broadcasters; and there was a German staff as well. The broadcasting was done in the Musikhalle, down the corridor from a tirade of nineteenth-century orchestral music. Furtwängler and Hindemith would come to conduct in the concert hall, and Gieseking, to my good fortune, would play the piano.

Shortly after I got there, I sent some of my usual wails back to Blighty, in letter form. This time, they concerned the Jonsonian spites and rivalries of a media environment. To the *déjà-lu* of one such complaint Robert Taubman responded in style, though with a hint of exhaustion:

> Many thanks for my half-share of your grief. I have passed the other half on to Hector, who received it with fortitude. I hope things have settled down better by now; you say so little about it that it's impossible to guess what's wrong with the Hamburg set-up, except that people are jealous of each other. O Karl, you who want to frequent the literary salons of London! Like Tiresias, you are learning to foresuffer all.

Before long, I had learnt to live with these sufferings.

I worked as an assistant to a padre from Ulster, Robert Crossett, a gruff, decent, distressed man, and an effective, emotive broadcaster. This meant that I travelled round Germany seeing to the transmission of church services. I also wrote reams of book and film reviews in an office whose windows gave onto an ancient red-light street. My grandmother had defined a brothel for me (one had been mentioned, in an access of candour, by Walter Scott) as 'a place where bad people go, and dance'. I asked: 'Is there a brothelle in Gilmerton?' Having yet to be told about the existence of the one beyond the back garden of my violin teacher's house, I had never been able entirely to believe in Scotch brothels: but here were authentic German ones. Spent from my church services, I would sit and watch the whores as they displayed themselves in shop windows of a sort, like so many second lieutenants, attended by maids in caps and aprons.

The head of the station was a civilian, Leslie Perowne, bright as a bird, a lover of opera and of bygone military uniforms, who'd been dispatched from the Gramophone Department of the BBC to spread the Spoken Word and the values of the Corporation. A neat captain, with a sharp look and a moustache you could shave with, warmed the hearts of Rhine Army with peripatetic human-interest shows. There was a cadre of disc-jockeys, one of whom was Chris Howland: he and his wife Kay were to become my friends. Another friend was Bombardier, then Corporal, Bill Utting, who was to achieve further promotion in civilian life – to the post of chief adviser to the Government on social services and social work. Betty Harvey-Jones was the queen of our drama productions; her husband John was at that time the Naval Attaché in Hamburg, and, at a later time, by far the most bohemian-looking chairman of ICI that it is possible to imagine. I am beholden to him for the gift of a copy of Daisy Ashford's *The Young Visiters*. He must have been reading my diary.

By now, I was back in my element, reading Proust in the evenings. I admired Orwell's *1984*, while making it sound, in a letter home, like a bowl of gruel – 'lumpy', 'frugally written'. It was also 'sick'. I listened a lot to Haydn's *Clock* Symphony, which seemed to chime me towards Cambridge. No one read comics. There was no more public hoisting of penises, no more virtuoso masturbation. There was, however, some consenting of adults in private. I was alerted to this when the soldiers in the unit staggered shambolically onto parade, at our barracks on the outskirts of the city, in uniforms that might have been slept in. There we all were, in brilliant disarray, a platoon of cissies and loitering, prejudicial Damons, a bunch of hyacinths in the Army's incredulous hand. A weary sergeant-major caused a convulsive movement by doing up a hip button, and roared out the arresting words: 'It's all right – my name's not So-and-so.' Naming one of his superior officers.

I was taken aback by some of this, and was Scottish about it, at first, in letters home. A local playwright's plays were 'all bad, homosexually bad. Oscar Wilde gone to hell'. Walks in pine forests, and by the beachy banks of the Elbe, with an English gentlewoman and two gentle German sisters, were an early intermission from the doings of the untoward soldiery. Of the *mulier generosa Anglica* – though without recourse to that seventeenth-century classification – I said in a letter: 'I do not worry that she's as cautious, amorously, as a pair of binoculars.'

We did look a bit like Dad's Army, and were almost as much a repertory company or a greenroom as we were a military unit. This unit was weak on insult and subordination. We refrained from grinding the faces of the Germans, and with some of them, as with these sisters, I became friends. I remember a Chekhovian doctor and his wife, making do with very little in a lonely house beyond the barracks, inhabitants of a city where districts still lay flat to the horizon after the air-raids of five years before. But it wasn't the case that features and drama and family favourites were the closest we came to soldierliness. We also served who drove through the Eastern Zone to Berlin in order to broadcast groaning hymns and not very godly sermons. I was even captured by the Russians. Our equipment was impounded at Helmstedt, on the border of the Eastern Zone. Standing between a portrait of Lenin and a portrait of Stalin, I was interrogated by an officer, an inoffensive one: he did not ask me if I knew what thought did. Consulting my documents, however, he did inquire why I had four names. My middle ones, Fergus Connor, coincided with a name from Britain's radical past, though I doubt whether that would have reassured him. Not that he really cared. The Cold War ran to such flurries. It was some while after the Berlin Airlift, but the Russians were still behaving in a regimental manner, so there had to be this charade that I might be smuggling in some second sapper, or Third Man, by means of an excess of names. The Germans with me were thrown into a camp for a week or two, then released.

The British Army of the Rhine was, by this stage, an anachronism. Its deterrent operations within the Nato context could as well have been conducted, by a wholly professional army, from bases in Britain, and the decision to maintain a presence in Germany was a mistake which may in part have issued from some obscure desire for the sensations of conquest. The Army's occupation of that country left many of its soldiers singularly unoccupied. Its presence there was like a piece of the expiring British Empire, complete with memsahibs and married families, awkwardly attached to the resurgences that were to become the German Miracle.

At a later time, while camping in Lancashire with the Territorial Army, I ran into the Scots friend from my first Hampshire hut. I was standing in a long queue outside a cookhouse tent, where the food was covered with a hundred thousand wasps. Round he came with his cane – just in case there were underlings to be thrashed. We had difficulty in penetrating our respective disguises, but we managed to speak a few embarrassed words. Then he walked away, having inspected the wasps, and that was the last I saw of him. The failure of communication here was only natural, given the way the Army went on. But the way the Army went on was to rankle in the minds of National Servicemen.

There were people I knew, from various walks of life, who set off after National Service to Cambridge and to Oxford, where they turned away from what was promised them, from advancement and opportunity, and indeed from merit, from the sort of virtue which is dead set on not being its own reward. In its more objectionable features, this promising ancient university struck them as rather like the Army: there was Robin, none other, sitting among the college silverware, being waited on. So they joined or rejoined the working class, speaking the language and dressing in rough textures and dark, dangerous hues. The attitudes of these dissenters were rarely to match any of the usual kinds of progressive politics, but they were shared by others of their generation, and may well have lent something of themselves to the more widely acknowledged drop-out that took over in the Sixties. They can be caught in a very good film that was made about National Service, *The Bofors Gun*: a bleak account of the anxieties of a boy who quits his unit in Germany to be an officer cadet. His anxieties remind me of my guilty eagerness to abscond to the microphones.

CHAPTER EIGHT

Rex Grantae

When, in 1951, I arrived in Cambridge to read for a degree in English, Mark Boxer had been there for a year and was already a star. At the beginning of that Michaelmas term his fame could be heard on the wind like some horn of Elfland as I went about in a gown buying my umbrella, kettle and bottle of sherry, and bearing a set of plain white Woolworth's mugs back to Downing College, to be painted in black lacquer with the names of poets. The embellishment was intended as a show of sensitivity which might both express and induce a bit of contempt when witnessed by the unsympathetic. Mark would never have been mug enough to be a namer of mugs, could never have made any such purchases (I was not long in regretting them), and would never have been seen dead in a gown on any but mandatory occasions. But the naughty little men and boys of his drawings of the time – a time when a college chaplain could be reported as saying that sex was a poorish thing, but suitable for 'that awkward hour between evensong and cocktails' – would have looked well on crock or urn, and he was later to design and decorate a cup. Taking it by its distinctive ear, you drank from the doubtful chalice of Prince Charles's head.

Struggling back to Downing with my kit, a Scottish scholarship boy half-persuaded of the rising-up before him of a Kafka's Castle of established airs and advantages – this made me different from Mark, though not as different as I may have imagined. Before long I was sitting with friends in Downing, engaged in the study of an undergraduate gossip column which teased a man called Cradock for the affected burns and leather patches on his sports jacket. Could this be our own Bob Cradock, whose burns and patches had already become a feature of college life? How had the Castle known of him? He had only just got here. We were then to be shamed by the discovery that this was a celebrated Percy Cradock, a leading University light. Many years later I met this light, at a point when glasnost had revealed him to have been an Intelligence supremo, an 'M'. Sir Percy's face was dark with the undisclosable. His suit was darker still. His spy's eye fell on me with what felt like suspicion. Perhaps he remembered me as the sort of Cambridge man he didn't greatly care to remember. For a moment there, I was back with the splendour that falls on castle walls.

I grew to like Cambridge, though, and soon lost my awe of it. It was a place in which to be young, where there were interesting people, where the heart might miss its beat, and you might throw yourself to the floor of your room in a fit of grief. It was a place from which you could walk out into a countryside at once ancient and innocent and fresh, with streams and trees and birds. Motorways had yet to sour the landscape. When I go there now, I have the sense that those were the last days of a happy marriage of town and country in that part of the world, a sense of the arrival of an American sameness, all malls, supermarkets and electronics factories. This may be age speaking. But I feel that in the Fifties Cambridge was still very much itself and as it had long been: austere, no doubt, at times class-bound and parochial, but on the whole a good place, or set of places.

I was astonished and a touch inflamed by the place that was given over to the worship of style, wit and panache, to a sexual intercourse of Restoration fops, romantic lovers, Brummells, Wildes, Sebastian Flytes, Lermontovs, *âmes damnées*; death's-heading it in their midst went the Leavisian man of principle and feeling. An archaic patricianism was about, mounting shows of sensitivity and snobbery. It could be said of someone that 'he knows everybody.' And nearly everybody was called Simon, or darling. The streets were a promenade of wits, dandies, sportsmen, barely parted from their public schools, even those of them who'd just been demobilised, and dressed in a weird exacerbation of Edwardian chic – pipe-stem tweed trousers, lapelled and brocaded waistcoats, wilting bow-ties, wafer-thin flat caps. There was even an escorting of Zuleikas. Beerbohm's old Varsity romance was still read; so were Forster's *The Longest Journey* and

Rosamond Lehmann's *Dusty Answer*, for their pictures of an amorous Cambridge on the eve of successive world wars. The smart set of the Fifties came to consist of people who'd escaped the second of these wars, were living at a comparatively peaceful and comfortable time, and were all for adventures, witty sayings, pretty sights. A female friend of Mark's said of an enemy set that the difference between 'them' and 'us' was that we were beautiful and they were not (Cocteau's film *La Belle et la Bête*, which speaks up for beasts, had been seen at the Arts Cinema). There was blasphemy in the remark, I felt. But I was stirred by such cheek.

A homosexual sub-culture had come into its own. Agents of the Homintern were thick on the ground, deep and crisp, and even good King Wenceslas was suspect. There were those who affected to be, but were really not, 'queer': pronounced 'quack' by the upper-class ducks on the pond. My eyes had opened in adolescence, rather late in the day, to the fact that the sexual liberation that seemed to be proceeding had extended its sanction to unnatural practices (in Cambridge, a visitor from what was left of Bloomsbury would in due course amuse by referring to some of these as more 'civilised' than others). Since then, friends, friends of friends, whole platoons and professions, had unmasked themselves as 'musical', to revive one of the relevant code-names. When I went to study in America, many of the friends I made there were gradually discovered to be musical too, most of them as yet secretly so, and I was told that such tastes had once proved orchestral in the Harvard Geography Department, and had caused it to be disbanded.

'Sometimes I think that all the world's a little queer, except for thee and me ... And even thee ...' The old joke sank in. Without dreaming that the incidence of unnatural practices would ever be anything like what it has been declared to be by statisticians in subsequent decades, I was aware that there was a lot of that going on, though you could not, I supposed, call it common: indeed part of its appeal, for someone like myself, a more or less unmusical someone, was that it was sectarian and subversive, both exhibitionist and clandestine, and that it was considered, by various kinds of expert, morbid and blasphemous. At the same time, I had long known that it was human, and that it ought not to be persecuted and proscribed. I relished the company of homosexual people, and I still relish the jokes and displays that date from the time when their behaviour was forbidden. A great beauty was heard to say of his spotted dog: 'It was given to mi by someone who loved mi very much, in Dalmatia.'

A man I'd liked when I was in the Army in Germany died during these years, and his male lover then committed suicide. At the inquest, the mother of this lover spoke of the loss of 'my son's very dear friend'. Her truthfulness made an impression on me, and it was one I was later to find myself transferring to my recollections of Cambridge. Playgrounds, as you might say, are no joke. In this Arcadia or Dalmatia of the Fifties the love of men for men – for all its larks and poses, between evensong and cocktails – was deadly serious for some, a life's work and a main hope, never to be outgrown. And there was death in this Arcadia too. A number of the friends I made there were to die before their time, as Mark himself did. The painter Rory McEwen was to develop cancer. Tony White died of a pulmonary embolism, after a football injury. Nick Tomalin, serving as a war correspondent, was killed by a heat-seeking missile in the Middle East. Bob Cradock, Sandy Cunningham and Rory's brother Robin also died before their time. And so did the American critics John Farrelly and Marius Bewley, both of them students and associates of Leavis.

I did not expect to become friendly with Mark, but I did, and we were to work together on the undergraduate magazine *Granta*. 'Miller has started to call people darling,' disapproved a Downing friend, who was later to lead a homosexual life. Downing could be quite as disapproving as its reputation alleged, and as its name alleged: here was another instance of the Helen Walker obligingness of language. For broadcasting on the BBC, I was one night ineffectually attacked – at some slight cost to my books – by the samurai of the college rugby club, who used to charge themselves up for such attacks – on Communists, pacifists and other deviants – by getting drunk at their annual feast. The leader on this occasion was a future expert on the works of D. H. Lawrence, who was drowned when swimming in the sea. Meanwhile at King's I had a friend who disapproved of Lawrence, and who eventually walked to a Lawrentian death in the Alps.

Mark was a study in green when I first remember meeting him. The suit he had on was the only questionable garment he was ever to wear, but he was pleased with it, while equally pleased that he had torn it climbing into King's after hours the night before. It was a time to be wearing green, which was in its salad days as the colour of the ecological crusade, but which also bore a lively, if comparatively esoteric, anthropological meaning locally. My teacher Leavis's wife, Queenie, had taken thenabouts to looking up in search of fertility symbols at the inn signs of East Anglia: which prompts me to say that Mark was a green king or knight who was notable for an olive, Sephardic beauty – mossy eyes, wavy hair, graceful limbs. He was stylishly good at the games learnt at his, so to speak, insufficiently famous public school, as well as at parties and drawing, and at drawing the guests at parties. He giggled, and – as if coached by Oxford's golden-shirted Ken Tynan, who was by now starring in London – he stammered in delivering his sayings and spites. It was right to stammer, as it was right to appear gay or versatile – to appear to be burning the candle at both ends, as one of his captions has some vicar or chorister say of a colleague. Both habits or appearances Mark was presently to abandon.

He could be the shy show-off who was willing to charm and disarm, and to wound. A recent autobiography has complained of his jealousy and hostility on *Queen* Magazine in London, but he was no threat to his companions on *Granta*, though he was sometimes cool and crossly efficient, and even Leavisianly severe. Some of us wanted to be very tough and London. One of us, Nick Tomalin, when asked about a copy date, glanced keenly at his wristwatch and replied: 'Next Thursday.'

Mark's commitment to the *jeunesse dorée* of his undergraduate years, and to smart sets in London, supplied the medium in which he did what he fancied doing; it was what he worked with; but it helped to shape him too. It was possible for some to suspect his charm, to scent design, and to know from books about the complicity of satirists with the objects of their derision: but his charm was seldom resisted or resented. Leavis would have been able to resist it, had a meeting been arranged. But there we were, many of us, delighted and attracted. His mother was or had been a Communist, as mine had been, after a fashion, and I liked that. There was between us, I found, an affinity as well as a disparity, and when he ran a photograph of me which was duly ascribed in Oxford to a reason of the heart, I was secretly better pleased than became a reader of Leavis's journal *Scrutiny*, which was then about to cease publication.

One afternoon we talked in the courtyard of King's. A fading summer sunlight lay on the colleges, making them more beautiful than any student cygnet or cynosure. He told me that a doctor had said there might be something wrong with him, a fault that might not go away, and he mentioned a fear that he might end up an object of pathos. A rumour on the subject of his health was to circulate, pointing to the doom that is assigned to talent, precocity and effrontery. He died in his fifties. By that time the pattern of early death among friends of mine of this generation had become apparent, and in one or two of the lives in question a suicidal strain had also become apparent.

Forebodings may have been sensed during the ceremonies that attended the mock-death of Mark's rustication or sending-down towards the end of his third and final year. A funeral procession halted in King's Parade, a matter of yards from where he had spoken of his illness; a coffin was shown to the multitude; and Mr Hugh Thomas, a President of the Union and in the fullness of time a Thatcher lord, clambered up beside it to declaim a valedictory oration.

Mark was exiled for printing in *Granta* a blasphemous poem by Anthony de Hoghton, an itinerant Catholic blue-blood, one of a series of visitors who were to trouble the peace and judgement of the Cambridge smart set (there was also a *faux-*Mitford in a British-warm officer's overcoat, who would remove it and stand about speechless yet strangely interesting at cocktail parties, until he made off with a clock from the University Arms Hotel and was revealed to be a member of the working class). I was *Granta*'s 'literary adviser', but as often happens with literary advisers, I was away when the poem was chosen for publication. It consisted of rough-tongued expostulations addressed to God: 'Get up out of bed, you rotten old sod' was the note. The poem could only have come from a man who, prone though he was to malicious practical jokes, was in some sense compelled by the question of faith. It was read in certain quarters, though, as a shocking insult. Shire clergymen sent in their thunders, and the University Proctors, mostly a Mr Prest, responded with Mark's dismissal and a suspension of the magazine. In a *Granta* lookalike which we brought out the episode was narrated in a strip cartoon by Rory McEwen. This took the form of a wonderful burlesque of the Bayeux Tapestry. Boxer, *Rex Grantae*, had roused the ire of the *sacerdotes Suffolkienses*, and hey presto, *Hic Prest se jactat contra Grantam*.

Rex Grantae came to no great harm. The sending-down was sent up, and there was a Pimpernel return for the May Balls which Mark might otherwise have disdained to grace. He also called on the University Appointments Board – about to be exposed in the *Spectator* as disliking Jewish students – and inquired, 'roguishly', he said, about jobs in the big world. With that, as the monks of Bayeux might have expressed it, *Rex Grantae se jactat ad Londinium*.

The sending-down was inflicted at a time when such penalties, such censorship, was the kind of thing that was only to be expected, which was also a time when students appeared to feel at home with Leavis's canon-building proscription of offensive literary works. The valedictory protest, however, may now, perhaps, be seen as a hint that times were changing, as a prelude to some of the protests and permissions, some of the easings-up, of the decades that followed. Not all of these freedoms – sounded out, on occasion, in festivity and play – are certain to last for ever. But it is as probable as most things are that the initiative so far as the chastisement of blasphemy is concerned has passed to the Moslem world, and that Britain's mullahs are not about to prevail on the country to introduce appropriate new penalties to its criminal code.

Granta was worth reading, I'd like to think, for all its excess of flair, and for all that it turned for a while into two magazines imperfectly related: one of them a proving-ground for stylish young men anxious to throw themselves at London, and into journalism and the theatre, the other solemn and literary-critical. The *Sunday Times* reported in 1954 that I 'must be the only editor *Granta* ever had who uses the word "wit" as a term of critical disparagement. The general intention seems to be the replacement of *Scrutiny*.' Those who worked on the paper, at one time or another, included Thom Gunn, Ted Hughes, David Gillies, John Coleman, Richard Mayne, Eric Hobsbawm, Ronald Bryden, Nick and Claire Tomalin, as they became, and Jonathan Miller, who became my brother-in-law.

Brilliant and keyed-up, Jonathan arrived on the scene with his foxy red head in a duffle hood and with sneakers on his feet. He had about him just a little of the wild boy of Aveyron, the eighteenth-century innocent in whom he was later to take an interest. This wild boy proved to be a scientist and a philosopher, and we would sit at his sneakers, feeling small, and faintly disgruntled, conscious of an innocence of our own. He was a comedian too – more of a comedian, I'd now say, than Danny Kaye, who was then held, by almost all, including me, to be very funny, and to whom at that point he bore a physical resemblance. His turns were a youthful ardour which gave the utmost pleasure – in conversation, on the stage and on the page. A *Granta* cartoon of his showed a grave old Grecian gent whose seat became a set of pram wheels. The caption read: 'God moves in a mysterious way.' This was the mirth of the scientist, for which I marvel that he wasn't sent down.

Ted Hughes was to become Poet Laureate, and the mainstay of an embarrassed Royal Family – a fate far from imminent in the poems of his which I published in an anthology, *Poetry from Cambridge 1952–4*, poems where forks are plunged into hot dishes, tusks are bloodied and a jaguar prowls. A quiet one, a charming bucolic piece called 'The Little Boys and the Seasons', has since gone uncollected – ranked, perhaps, among his juvenilia.

The magazine was Mark's début, or overture. Among my souvenirs is a careful letter of criticism directed by him at a lush story of mine which we carried. The story was entitled – before an 's' dropped out at the printer – 'Heads of Hair', and it could be said to share a preoccupation with John Gray's poem, lusher still, about extravagant manes, which I had yet to read. It presented the valedictions of a demon barber, whose original I had listened to while waiting for a haircut in his shop on Jesus Lane. James was a demon for the golden oarsmen and Adonises of the past – slain in wars but never to be forgotten – and for sherry with the Master of St Christopher's and his lady.

The story was one long purple passage, and was overexplained by the first-person narrator. There were too many words. Mark's criticisms were vigilant, those of the intervening sort of editor, and I would have done better to heed more of them than I did. The climax came when James moved to commemorate some superb Simon or other who had fallen, as Simons will, into disgrace, and whose mane had been Heseltinian. A vicar in the barber's chair asks if the fellow is now dead.

'Worse than dead,' countered James. Earnestly withholding the crime, he supplied the coda to this music of remembrance. 'He was the idol of the colleges, they used to say, the rose of the university, an athlete, a scholar, an everything, sir. Oh what a lovely gentleman! Oh what a lovely gentleman! And what a magnificent head of hair!'

James's assistant then identifies himself as the disgraced man.

Mark's letter might in part have come from a more or less roguish custodian of English usage: ' "Done" is a northernism, I am sure!' As in the age of Samuel Johnson, the northernism was removed in favour of a more acceptable expression: 'But the hero James had just finished celebrating ...' Mark's chief concern, however, was the ending. It was a weakness that 'the assistant exposes himself with *you* there.' He was right – and the identification should have been left to surmise. The letter finishes, I should add, 'done' being a northernism, with the entreaty: '*Please* don't be cross.'

This was a camp or rococo version of one of the transactions that helped to make Cambridge worthwhile. Those of the young who wanted to write wrote, and showed each other what they'd been doing. A great pleasure of the place was to watch Thom Gunn, of the sounding, crashing laugh and lumberjack shirts, become a poet. Poems would arrive as items in his letters; the place itself was in those poems, his friends' predicaments and his own. I think I am right in remembering that one of them was meant to teach me the lesson that I should pull myself together. It said that I was a soul in vacuous torment – as indeed I sometimes was. Soul should be 'mastered', and seen as 'blood'.

> Your house is haunted. Up and down the stairs
> Hurtles a sheeted thing that moans and shrieks . . .

At the start of 1953 a letter from Kent spoke of 'eight new poems since I saw you, and no signs yet of weakening. The Spring.' Nevertheless, 'if one can find the slightest reason for being sad one will be . . . I woke up about 2, last night, & heard a cock crowing; thought of the bare ploughed fields all round the house; desperate loneliness. Self-pity, you see, rampant.' I saw. He then went on to mention a plan for 'a verse novel! In *six* books!!'

I was full of admiration for what he was up to with his poems and plans.

> Shall I be John a Gaunt and with my band
> Of mad bloods pass in one spectacular dash,
> Fighting before and after, through your land,
> To issue out unharmed the farther side
> With little object other than panache
> And showing what great odds may be defied?

This was followed in my anthology by a different Gunn:

> I thought I was so tough,
> But gentled at your hands
> Cannot be quick enough
> To fly for you and show
> That when I go I go
> At your commands.

At Cambridge he found himself, body and soul. He came to know there what he was, and to know that he wished to be what he was. This was to mean, for his poems of the time, that while gentleness had its place, self-pity was out. 'Brute purpose' received its due. History's 'toughs' were scandalously praised, and preferred to Stephen Spender's 'truly great', thought-of continually. Belt-buckle and jeans were in, and by those who felt as Thom did, Mark, though he was liked, could be judged effeminate, and sartorially unsound. 'Panache' was a word and a mode of the time and place, and its prince was Tony White, saluted as a local avatar, a fine ideal of tender toughness. Thom's Cambridge poems, plain-spoken and robust, rapidly caused him to be credited to the Movement school in London: but the romantic and the existentialist in them imposed a distance, and he was never to settle in that gallery. As rapidly, he left for America, and a new life.

Towards the end of the swinging Sixties another scene was played out in the late sunlight of a summer afternoon. I went to have a drink with Mark and his wife Arabella at their house in London, in Holland Park, hoping to persuade him to take up drawing again after an interval of years spent as the editorial director of magazines. I was editing the *Listener*, and we agreed to start a strip there based on the trendy home life of a media couple, the String-Alongs. Before long, the couple felt imaginary, autonomous. At the same time, the strip took traits from friends, some of whom figured among the talking-head geniuses and pebble-glassed thrusters of the television programmes and colour-supplements of the day. The reliance on friends brought a compunction I still feel, and made the strip denounceable as harbouring the in-house acerbities of the Cambridge Mafia then suspected of dominating the media. My favourite image is that of the male String-Along hanging from his ceiling in a basket chair, his horn-rims trained on a treatise by R. D. Laing.

Mark's line relaxed as it matured; the sharpness and stiffness to be seen in some of the *Granta* drawings of his time at Cambridge were to disappear. His early work was influenced by Steinberg and by Haro Hodson. Osbert Lancaster's influence then began to matter, or to matter more, and Mark eventually undertook emulous pocket cartoons in newspapers. His line became suppler and softer, fuzzy and feathery and faint at times, altogether more adventurous, with a wider range of tones and effects and with nice patches of bold black. Early and late, there was a tension in his work between décor and satire, artist and journalist. He did not stand all that close to Lancaster's mastery of social comment, verbal and visual: the words he coined and commissioned for his balloons and captions were a secondary element in what he did.

When the String-Along strip appeared in the *Listener*, it gave the necessary initial offence, though it was neither blasphemous nor unequivocally permissive. It might even have been thought by some to be a rebuke to the licentious new modes that had come about. And yet the strip was at least as much an expert's or connoisseur's manual of design and costume, a guide to the new decorum, as it was a mockery of those people who worried about such matters. It was, as satire often is, a form of self-satire. What was the standpoint from which the String-Alongs were to be reckoned divertingly obnoxious: socialism, Old Money, blue blood, that of a wholesome country gentry, together with such friends of theirs as the *sacerdotes Suffolkienses* – a gentry that might be held to have something in common with the one invented by Evelyn Waugh in order to put down the upstarts and media people of the Twenties? Mark was and remained a man between worlds, both Figaro and the Count, just as his art hesitated between elegance and mischief. Old Money and blue blood had some poisonous things to say about him behind his back, and they would no doubt have been happy to confuse him with the String-Alongs.

Like Waugh, he was more of a media man than his satire was angled to suggest.

The BBC's chiefs, entrusted with the task of keeping an eye on the *Listener*, were inclined to frown on the strip when it began. In the lift at Broadcasting House I was greeted with a wintry smile by a proctorial member of the Board of Management, who managed to convey that, as a cultivated man himself, he'd be sorry if we were to be sent down. This was a gentleman's nod and wink, rather than the conduct of someone sworn to the suppression of immorality. But I couldn't help recalling the hint several years later, when, with Mark better-known to the nation, the Board of Management said yes to a programme in celebration of his talents, which proved to be one of British television's totally admiring and consenting portraits of the artist.

CHAPTER NINE

Passionate Will

'Let's go over to the smart side of the room,' an undergraduate suggested to me once, rather pointedly, at a party in Fifties Cambridge. The human deficiencies of the smart were not hard to detect. They were part of the point. Their audacities, one supposes (one kept saying 'one' at this time), were mainly directed at God, and can't have done much human harm. At the time of the 1984 miners' strike, I saw a card, printed by some Cambridge students, which employed the language of the strike's supporters in inviting the Simons of the day to celebrate 'the destruction of the mining communities of the North'. To this display Thatcherism had lent a measure of sanction and protection, and an edge of nastiness. The shows and snobberies of Fifties Cambridge were, in comparison, benign, or, as some might prefer to say, seldom as shamefully funny. It is also true that, even with such interest as attached to the undergraduate magazines in their vicinity, they were no more than a corner of university life. Elsewhere people were reading for their degrees, and discovering the double-helix structure of DNA.

I remained sympathetic to Leavis's ideas, some of which were trained like guns on the fashionable Cambridge that he referred to as King's, and there was no defection, on my part, from Downing to 'King's'; when I moved to another supervisor in my third undergraduate year, it was in an attempt to broaden my studies, and it was to the girls' college of Girton that I went, to commune with Muriel Bradbrook. The battle between Leavis and his enemies had escalated by now to the proportions of a national engagement. The London reviewer Raymond Mortimer claimed that Leavis's prose was that of 'the Straffen of English literature'. Straffen was an atrocious murderer of the time.

I was, and have remained, in more than one mind about Leavis. He sometimes plays the kind father in my filial dreams, in a species of dream where the Queen also serves a sentimental purpose. In both cases, relations are good. I think that the Queen fancies me, and on one occasion she let me into her palace by the back door. This experience of Leavis, however, misrepresents the relations which obtained between us at the time. I was not among those who were close to him, a closeness which was liable to end in tears. He tended to distrust success in examinations, and I began to do well enough in exams for him to see in me the fault of 'journalistic facility'. I took against his way of promoting his opinions, and against the obedient acceptance of his exclusions and asperities – by students, for instance, who were unable to appreciate the distress that lay behind them. And I was put off by the School of Leavis which was establishing itself in the schools and universities of Britain and in the universities of America. My two minds and more brought it about that when I first became an editor, I was disliked by members of the London literary world as a Leavisian zealot and by Leavisian zealots as a renegade who had sold out to the London literary world. Then, during the decades that followed, he was to be scorned by new generations of zealot, whose adversarial prig behaviour resembled that of some of his own followers in earlier times. These followers have meanwhile been notably silent, for the most part, about his fall from favour. One or two have become his detractors.

J. B. Priestley was to say of me that, like Leavis, I 'hated literature'. Leavis loved it, I am sure, and knew what it was. He was a very good reader of literary texts, who wrote well about what good readings entail and may achieve. Good readings were both solitary and social, both diagnostic and dialectical – responsive both to the writer and to the readings of others, though he himself was often to prove unable to tolerate the ones he disagreed with. Good readings were a 'discipline of thought' and a kind of knowledge. In proceeding to claim for literary study a place at the centre of the intellectual life of the University, however, he could sometimes seem to be suggesting that literary students need no other knowledge, no recourse to other disciplines, to history or philosophy. Had he looked into the mirror here, he might have seen the face of those historians and philosophers of the present century who have refused to heed the evidence of imaginative literature. He persuaded many readers of my generation that literature was for everyone, including inhabitants of the mining communities of the North, while conceding far too much to the dialectical opposite, while persuading himself that only an élite composed of English gentlemen could be considered good readers.

When, on the road to Downing, I read his first book, *New Bearings*, which appeared in the year of my birth, I was roused by its talk of an intelligent and wide-ranging poetry which abhorred the tunnel vision of the self-pitying romantic singleton, which abhorred me and my smocked and sandalled love. The 'distinguished' poets known to him in 1931 were writing this poetry, and it was defended and justified at every turn. His contributions to the traditional cult of the great writer were to help to set the terms for his own ascendency. In that sense, he was his own master: but he had to have other masters too, and to change them in the course of his career. I was at ease with these contributions, and with the cult itself. Reading in his book about Eliot and Pound, I did not think to ask – any more than Lotte's friend Wolf Mankowitz did in his essay in *Scrutiny* on Eliot's poem 'Gerontion' – if great writers could be anti-semites and snobs.

When I reread the book in 1990, I found in it, still, a strong defence of Modernist writing. But I had tired of the great writer who always has to be defended and exalted, and I found that there were arguments which brought some discomfort. In *New Bearings* Victorian poets are said to have suffered from an emotional debility which caused them to withdraw into a dream world not unlike the one in which Leavis was later to be kind to me. The 'stress of cerebral muscle' was absent from their work. Soon afterwards, however, they are said to have been unlike the Georgian poets in possessing a 'robust, full-blooded emotional confidence'. Browning, indeed, is faulted for having too much of that. Leavis deals with the difficulty that may have been suspected at this point by declaring that the exercise, on

Browning's part, 'of certain grosser cerebral muscles' was not the same thing as the play of intelligence in poetry. Browning was coarse. He was an 'inferior' mind. Eliot, though scarcely to be seen, even then, as full-blooded, was both cerebral and intelligent.

By the time I reached Downing a painful disillusionment and resentment had set in. 'Mr Eliot is the saint of letters no more,' I told them in Edinburgh. He was blamed for reneguing on Leavis's 'demolition' of Milton – a poet with whom Leavis might have been expected to have been distinctly in sympathy. Blake and Lawrence became his teachers, and Dickens was promoted from entertainer and inferior mind to great writer. Mockery of these changes of approach has been overdone, but was not surprising, given the dogmatic severity with which the old pre-eminences had been asserted, with which branch lines had been closed down in favour of an arterial great tradition. Leavis went on, in fact, to argue with considerable success, at times, on behalf of his changes of approach. The long late essay on *Four Quartets* examines the 'air of meaning', the 'spectral' explicitness, the 'quasi-logical' progression, which he finds in the poem. It identifies a 'something wrong', a plight, a revulsion and fear, a desire to withdraw from the 'human world'. No one would call this a friendly account. But it is not an account which is disrupted by the jealousy and hurt, the 'degrading meanness', which have been attributed to Leavis's writings.

Leavis could in person be courteous and funny, though you would not guess it from his reputation. He made Johnsonian jokes: of a colleague's book on Lawrence, 'to read it would be to condone it.' But his humour and his appetite for irony were apt to fail him when it came to what gave him pain or stirred his rancour. He was not at his funniest when he said how pleased he'd once been to be digging his garden when William Empson called, and therefore – in an exercise, perhaps, of the 'urbanity' he valued – unable to shake his hand. Nor was he amused by much of what was thought amusing. I once spoke to him about the Weekend Competitions run on literary subjects by the *New Statesman*, an enemy. He deplored them for a bit, and I chose to be bold and said that all the same they were amusing. Well yes, he replied, they might be *amusing*. Before long, I was in charge of these competitions – an outcome he would have held to be, in a favourite phrase, 'highly characteristic' of me. I won't deny that there were moments, while sifting the parodies and squibs, when I was able to see his point.

At Downing I had a hand in running the Doughty Society, which met to hear papers, few of which were delivered by Lord David Cecil. Wolf Mankowitz, busy in London with his novels and screenplays, agreed to give a talk: it was to be about job prospects for those with sensibilities, and to be called 'How to be Literate and Still Live'. At the last minute a telegram of cancellation arrived, which alluded to a now forgotten panjandrum of the British film industry: 'Pressure of film work intolerable – J. Arthur Mankowitz.' As an officer-bearer, I sighed. As a human being, I was amused. I peered at my master's brown face as he read the telegram I had slyly shown him. 'Highly characteristic of Mankowitz,' he pronounced.

There is a political content to the Leavis story. Here were the endurance of exclusion, the overthrow of entrenched authority, a leadership which suspected and expelled associates and insisted on adherence. It wasn't altogether chimerical to glimpse in what went on the perfect people of some old puritan enclave, some 'blessed remnant', blaming and being blamed. This was an elect or élite for whom other people were enemies, inferiors and, at best, innocents. According to a television play by Nigel Williams, Sir Arthur Quiller-Couch was an innocent sponsor of Leavis who was turned by the bitterness of Queenie Leavis's heart into an enemy; my own recollections are that Leavis would speak well of 'Q', as of a type of the English gentleman, while deriding his *Oxford Book of English Verse*. Such could be the intricacies of the Leavisian politics, which were premised for the most part on a black and a white. A mantra of enemy faults was recited. Homosexuality at King's was sneered at, while that of adherents went unnoticed or unremarked.

Pacing the sands in his sky-blue swimming-trunks at Dinard in Normandy, where he was staying with John Farrelly, formerly a journalist on the *New Republic* magazine in America, Leavis described his wife as 'the embodiment of passionate will'. When I first met Queenie Leavis at one of her tea-parties, she greeted me with the statement that the Highland half – or was it the whole? – of eighteenth-century Scotland was barbarous, and she was always to be very free with charges of barbarism and delinquency. Kingsley Amis was a pornographer, Angus Wilson a women's magazine hack: to remember these statements is to be repelled by them, as by many similar displays of an intolerance, shared with her husband, of the efforts of almost all recent writers. Films were barbarous, she held in the Fifties, and female undergraduates, in any case undesirable in their current numbers, were going to them as much as twice a week. This was before she discovered that there could be such things as serious films – among them, *Jules et Jim*.

The Leavises' book on Dickens, of 1970, has a chapter by her on *Bleak House*, which explains that Dickens 'is very often less simple-minded than his critics, especially those outside the English tradition and in such a brutally crude one as the modern American'. She believed herself heir to a superior English tradition which relegated modern America to barbarism. The chapter propounds a 'serious view' of Dickens, and opens with the words: 'There have been two main grounds for dismissing Dickens altogether as a novelist – that is, from serious consideration as a novelist, as something other than a successful entertainer (at which no one disputes his eminence).' Twenty years before, with an unintelligible exception made for *Hard Times*, F. R. Leavis had attempted just such a dismissal.

Q. D. Leavis was an able historian of nineteenth-century English literature and a journalistically skilful polemicist. But she made far too much, together with her husband, of the idea of an English tradition which was superior, yes, but gravely endangered by the emergence of an industrial society due to succumb to a predatory commercialism: not even the Leavisian true believer, strong against machines, advertising, entertainment and the masses, can always have felt entirely happy with this version of the fall of man. The claims made for her work, and the talk of neglect, have tended to ignore her limitations. It can't be trivial that she should have gone on in this injurious way, or that her use of the word 'serious' should have been so trivial. Her part in the formation and fate of the *Scrutiny* group is likely to have been as destructive as it was undoubtedly important, and it may be that Leavis's wounds were made worse by hers. She was said to have been cut off by her family for marrying outside the Jewish community, and there can never have been any lack of occasion thereafter for the exercise of her passionate will. Struggles between man and wife would seem to have been part of their agonistic close accord.

When he lay in his coffin at Eden Lilley's, the Cambridge store, she is thought to have visited him. Leavis was sometimes to leave Cambridge, his native place, where his father had kept a music shop: he left it for service as a medical orderly in the first war, for a walk in France, I have been told, with Aldous Huxley, for the beach at Dinard, a trip to brutal America, an appointment in old age at the University of York. But he was the most local of men, and this last scene, so far as it can be imagined, seems to say that, while seeming quite unlike any scene which it would make sense to call parochial. It also speaks of a common cause, and of its exactions.

The Leavises' later years have been discussed in two essays by Robert Houghton, who was an 'intense admirer of Leavis's work' when he was a Cambridge undergraduate. 'Before my exams at university,' William Donaldson has recalled, in the person of one of his comic characters, with reference to the Leavis of the Fifties, 'I wrote his finest insights on my cuffs. I came down unhonoured, but my shirts were awarded a good 2:1.' Houghton arrived a few years after this time, so far as there ever was quite such a time. The first of his essays appeared in the *Cambridge Quarterly* in 1988, and deals with 'the Leavises in the Sixties and Seventies'. The second appeared in the *London Magazine* two years later, and concerns a pupil of Leavis's who taught at Downing and then at the University of Kent. The essay is entitled 'Morris Shapira and the Downing English School'.

Morris Shapira, who was a friend of mine, is brought to life in this admiring portrait by Houghton, who used to eavesdrop on his supervisions at Canterbury. In 1966 there was a quarrel, during which Leavis 'disowned the *Cambridge Quarterly* and lied about his association with it – in print, if I remember rightly. Anyway he lied.' But 'Mrs Leavis was the essential liar.' Morris Shapira 'saw Leavis as having to choose between his wife and his friends and associates . . . To Morris he used to confide the terrible stresses she put him under; she knew he talked about her, so she distrusted and broke with friend after friend of his.' About some lesser matter, Morris told Houghton: 'Perhaps I just lied to you.' At Kent, Morris is said to have suffered from 'inferior' colleagues. Some of the students who visited him were 'coarse, some dirty'. Their condition is related to 'an area of darkness' in him, which had to do with his sexual desires. Morris was later to be murdered by a chance acquaintance.

In the earlier essay Mrs Leavis is warmly portrayed. She supervised Houghton, advising him to 'jot down critical ideas as they occurred to me. She had once lost an important insight through failure to do this.' The insight was important, but she could not remember what it was: this is not unlike Houghton's imparting that Morris, who was to publish virtually nothing, was the most important of Leavis's students, while relieving himself of the task of making clear what his importance consisted in. At Cambridge, the writer was made indignant by 'a middle-aged French lady employed to help me with the French set books. She shamelessly digressed and flirted.' Mrs Leavis did neither. But 'although she was nearly sixty, her dark eyes, with meltingly soft irises, were beautiful' and diffused 'a tender thoughtfulness'.

He returned to Cambridge to visit her in 1977. 'Leavis suffering from degeneration of the brain cells due to old age. Mercifully he was upstairs and did not join us, though he could be heard walking up and down above, up and down the stairs, and standing behind the door of QDL's sitting-room, no doubt listening to see if I was still there.' Mrs Leavis let Houghton know that her husband, in his last state, had been heard to say two things: '*I am wretched. I am in despair.*'

The essay says that this was Leavis *ex tenebris*, and the language is like that which has been used of the religious reprobate: the same words are used of Hogg's justified sinner at the conclusion of his novel. Houghton suggests that 'the attempt to live one's life, especially "religiously", largely in and through literature must fail,' and that Leavis's last state was due, not just to illness and old age, but also to this commitment of his to a religious view of literature, which caused him to fail at the art of living. Spoken like a Leavis, and like those of his disciples, as they were invariably called, who found what they needed in his wounded and wounding severity.

Of a 'disciple' of William Godwin, Hogg's contemporary, Hazlitt, wrote: 'his feeling of what is right is to be at all times wrought up to a pitch of enthusiastic self-devotion.' Houghton's feeling of what is right enables him to speak in this unusually severe way about people he once admired, and to end by saying that a number of Leavis's disciples have ended up in the same apocalyptic darkness as their master. 'One sees reckless idealism, failures to make provision for viable careers, eccentricity, collapsed lives, alcoholism, depression, desperate living, disaster, and madness.'

There were times, during my years at Cambridge, when Cambridge was almost all I could think of. I remember trying, in July 1952, after my first academic year, to take the measure of what had been happening. I was in Edinburgh, and the long vacation yawned. In diaryese: 'The solitude of these infinite spaces terrifies me.' Edinburgh seemed empty. Norman was in sight of Suilven. Hector was off on a school trip, having repaired his stock of friendships: 'Sir Bedivere is travelling in company.' As for that first year, I had made friends, and the kind of things that Leavis made me think had been grafted without pain to what I was already thinking. 'The Nether Fields' had been published in a university magazine, and the editor had warned me, misreading his Cambridge, about the possible impact of its somewhat factitious homosexual element. I had been assaulted by rugby-players. I had been denounced by parents who had intercepted and memorised my letters to their daughter. I had sat down and written them the letter of a manly man of feeling which might have been composed by Burns in his Sylvander mode, and the friendship had never recovered.

Early in the year I had met Dylan Thomas, when we turned up at an outside broadcast in a hall near Cambridge to play word games for the BBC. His word for a collection of undergraduates: 'a falutin'. He looked just like that Florentine putto. On this occasion as on others, I found in him a quality of good manners which rarely figures in the memorials of his life. I thanked him for his poems, and he replied: 'I hope they'll be better.' He seemed if anything a little demure, as a visitor to Cambridge then, on his guard against the literary critical comments and toffs' to-do's of that ancient university; the crisis of his last months and American lionising had yet to break, though it was not far-off. This was hardly the wild rover who'd excelled himself in some of the stories told about him in Edinburgh, hardly the author of lines attributed to him by Hector which you could call the limerick of my dreams:

> The night that I slept with the Queen
> She said as I whispered *Ich dien*:
> 'This is royalty's night out,
> So please switch the light out.
> The Queen may be had but not seen.'

Later on in Cambridge I was to tell him that one of a falutin of rugby-playing students, a man who lived in a castle near his boathouse in Wales, had referred to a girl I knew, reckoned by him to be a bohemian, as 'all right for sex'. Dylan Thomas kept repeating the phrase, in disapproving wonder, as if he were broadcasting on the Third Programme, and as he was also to do with the name Mau-Mau. I had never known such a way with words, such a tasting and mumbling. They were his girl-friends.

The infinite spaces of the summer of 1952 were soon enclosed in the nutshell of a Territorial Army camp near Morecambe, which re-introduced me to the real Army, as distinct from the greenroom adjunct of the Hamburg months. These Territorial

stints were regrettable, but they had their moments. The following year in the Highlands I was invited to the parlour of a Girl
Guide mistress who turned out to be running a disorderly house
– as far as I could see, as I sat on chatting in the parlour with
Akela. I was lying the night after in a hillside tent when a man
from Mull walked by with the words: 'The splendid gaieties of
Parisian sexual life are in no way to be compared with the
humdrum fuckeries of Findhorn.' It seemed that there was less
of the sexual revolution in all this than there was of the Ball of
Kirriemuir – that I might have stumbled on the survival of a
great Scottish tradition.

From Morecambe I moved to Normandy, to stay at Dinard
with John Farrelly and his wife – subsequently, and surprisingly,
to go off and live with George Barker, who had been heard to
say of Marius Bewley that rigor Leavis had set in. The Leavises
had just paid their visit there – too early in the season for them
to have had the pleasure of meeting a Dublin girl whom I
approached in one of the night spots. *Voulez-vous danser avec moi?*
Barrault's invitation to Arletty in *Les Enfants du Paradis*. She was
sorry but she didn't speak French; nor had she heard of Yeats.
This was no Norman conquest. She was to throw holy water on
me, and to say that I was 'a divel for crossing streets'. She was a
delightful Irish rose, whom Queenie Leavis would have taken to
be a savage.

Leavis had gone to the trouble of writing me out, during this
holiday of his, a Conrad reading list: *not*, it read, *Lord Jim*, and
not a number of other works. 'And there are one or two poor
collections of short stories.' This, it could be said, was his way
of liking Conrad. The list referred to the surgery entailed by his
efforts to make the most of the English moralist in Conrad's
fiction.

Back in Cambridge, I began to see more of the bohemian girl
mistakenly thought to be all right solely for sex. 'For Mary who
does not smoke, from John who burns.' The present-giver was
John Coleman, but it was I who burned, not Coleman, and
Mary is not her real name. Coleman was also to address her, as
'Streak-head', in a poem of disdain, 'To an Unfortunate Lady',

where this non-smoker and non-knitter is seen to toy, for a stanza, with a ball of wool and a fag:

> Your cigarette can weave
> Great patterns for the fool
> Who's willing to believe
> What glows may not be cool.
>   He'll do to hold your wool.

I held her wool, and I did not care a bean, as she used to say, that Morris Shapira was less impressed with her looks than I was. There was a round pale face to be impressed with, tawny hair, Russian cheeks, a bottle-green Circassian jacket out of Lermontov, various effects of jade and Chinese white. She wanted 'to be loved' by me, but only sometimes wanted it, and not enough for my peace of mind. My interest in authors was still unslaked, and I was interested to be told that her father, a sardonic bearded Bloomsbury gentleman sage who might almost have been thought to move in a mysterious way, had ridden in a carriage through the Italian night with Ronald Firbank, who had exclaimed: 'Oh what a beautiful moon! Oh what a beautiful moon! You're *my* moon.' My own moon was not to prove auspicious. Early in the friendship I set down 'a presentiment of disaster, defeat'.

The day before that, in a practical criticism seminar, Leavis had perused a letter he'd received from America. The handwriting was old-fashioned and the writer a somebody James. 'You write just like my Uncle Henry,' Leavis was informed. 'I don't mind saying,' said the critic of Henry James, 'that I think that's an exceedingly pleasant letter.' The youths of the seminar looked on respectfully, glad of a break from worrying whether Hardy's 'And the unseen waters' ejaculations awe me' was a good line.

Leavis could, as on this occasion, be charming. His explosive French made his rendering of the name Rémy de Gourmont a match for MacDiarmid's 'aggrandise'. But this Francophile could be sharply critical of the French – of their levity, in particular. 'As for the French,' he exclaimed, 'I could kick them' – and his foot jerked out in a little stab. 'As for love,' said Marius Bewley, who preferred the comradeship of Greek warriors setting out together for battle, 'it was one of those ideas that gat going with the French.' And American Marius was to argue in *Scrutiny* that Henry James owed less to French than to English literature.

At the end of that Michaelmas term a party of undergraduates went to France, where Mary was set to meet an older man, a painter, an Existentialist, whose arrival was, in the event, from my point of view, agreeably deferred. Pride forebade me to join them, and I took off to burn in Edinburgh, where I was helping with the mails once again, at Waverley Station, whose ancient lift had 'chopped a couple of laddies' heads off and squeezed a big fat woman flat'. I was dozing by the fire in the postmen's room when I spotted a fairy – a green, misty translucent thing the size of a small frog, which vanished when a postman's boot clumped past. But then I didn't believe in fairies; affectation had coaxed this one into sight. 'Such is the extraordinary power of sentiment at that age,' as Anthony Powell says in one of his novels.

In the Abbotsford pub an English art critic told me, not wholly to my dismay, that he'd known an 'arty and kittenish' Mary in the unimaginable before. In another pub Hector told me to pull myself together, and to bear in mind Shaw's advice about abandoning yourself to a mighty purpose. I did not think to retort that Shaw's mighty purposes had included Stalin. His principles obliged him to support Stalin's mighty purposes. But he found fault with the devotion to principle which prevents Jeanie Deans from telling her lie. I have some sympathy with him there.

During my second year as a student I occupied a room in a good-looking gloomy house by the back door of Downing and across the street from a mortuary. Built by the Downing architect, Wilkins, the house belonged to Henry Morris, deviser of the Cambridgeshire system of 'village colleges', and a touchy landlord, more than capable of thrusting undesirables into the street, if not the morgue – among them, at one point, William Empson and the officials of the undergraduate English Club, which he'd been addressing that evening in the disguise of a cold squire from Yorkshire. The disguise was to be observed and reported in later times, but I was never to see it again myself when I came to know him better, and to be all for him in his rich idiosyncrasy and zeal: 'I must keep hurrying on.'

The Ouse flooded in the new year, and I went off one morning to do a self-conscious good work by filling sandbags with mud. I returned to my room to find Mary, no less charitably disposed, but with her 'flair for the non-committal' intact. How was I to express this trouble, having 'emitted such a sad variety of groans since I first kept diaries'? I had applied to it the technique of exaggeration greatly overdone in the diaries, with their pre-emptive imagining of the worst. But now it seemed for a while as if the worst had come. I had turned into Thom Gunn's 'sheeted thing that moans and shrieks'.

I found a text in the Bible, in Proverbs, which fitted the case: 'He knows not that the dead are there and that her guests are in the depths of hell.' Here too there was exaggeration, and a certain freedom of interpretation: the Bible was referring to a disorderly house, like, or not very like, the one up there in the Highlands. I would have done better to take my text from John Coleman, that evident contemporary of the disconsolate Philip Larkin. Coleman had had this to say:

> In legend-land, through light crepuscular
> the Princes move, all highly muscular:
> my vault across love's padded horse
> is doomed to drop half-way, of course.

I had by now made friends with Rory McEwen, who was reading English and who came from the Borders, where I was sometimes to stay with his family. That summer I went to Bardrochat in Ayrshire, where their holidays were spent: a Lorimer house that looks across a valley to the summit of Arthur's Seat-like Knockdolian, with Ailsa Craig in the distance out at sea and the cannibal cave of the ogre Sawney Bean down by the seashore. At Christmas I set off across the Moorfoots from Gilmerton – where my simple uncle had been skirmishing with my simple aunt – to stay at Marchmont. The McEwens were Catholics. There were six brothers and a sister, kilted

Kisty. Their father was a Conservative politician, their mother
might have put you in mind of an Allan Ramsay portrait of the
Princesse de Clèves: the living breath, as I was bound to think,
of aristocratic composure, an astute woman with a strong will
and a ripe sense of caste. Perhaps she was astute enough to
guess, as I now can't, the reason for my Christmas present to her
– a copy of *Women in Love*. I can't have been trying to proselytise
on behalf of the sexual revolution, though it was plain that there
were sections of the Border gentry which had completely ignored
its message. A recent bride of Lammermuir was said to have
telegraphed her mother on the day after her wedding: 'I'm
coming back. Johnny's gone mad.'

The house at Marchmont is the work of William, father of
Robert, Adam, and was built by the Lord Marchmont who was
a friend of the poet Pope. Pope once remarked of his own
juvenile verse that it was begotten on 'innocence' by 'self-love':
and now innocence and self-love had come to Marchmont. The
house is of local stone, preferred to exotic ashlar, and is all the
finer for rising up in a dignity of pink Border rubble, encircled
by rhododendron beds. The Merse is Hume country. One of
these Humes was presently to become prime minister. Another,
le bon David, the philosopher, had been censured in his youth by
the Chirnside presbytery for misconduct with a servant girl.
And Alexander Hume had sung the praises of the Merse in a
magnificent poem of the later Middle Ages, the itemising of an
entranced summer's day.

> All trees and simples great and small,
> That balmy leaf do bear,
> Nor they were painted on a wall,
> Na mair they move or stir.

These lines foretold what Rory was to do: he would paint
pictures of leaves and hang them on walls, having begun by
painting roses and carnations in the manner of the French
master Redouté and with the touch of a monkish illuminator, a
touch as different from my father's as a statement is from a
mood, a fixed point from a flux.

At Cambridge he did portraits on vellum of Neal Ascherson and myself. The tiny brush-strokes produced a good, somewhat African likeness of Neal, who had come to Cambridge from the Marine Commandos, went about in jungle-green with a Thai girlfriend, and kept an inscrutable piece of weaponry on his hearthrug at King's. He was himself inscrutable. Baffled by his 'sported oak' or closed outer door, a wag was said to have slid beneath it a note: 'I came to see you, but you were in.' The wag may also have experienced some difficulty in finding him out. Neal's gifts as a writer and thinker, and as a shape-changing self-creator, were not lost, however, on those who took up with him at this point.

Having gone to school and university in England, he was to embrace his Northern antecedents and to become a romantic socialist Scotsman, who wrote his articles for a time in Edinburgh. He even learnt the language. A Scotsman of the mind, is Neal, the ideal Scotsman – who is also subject to recognition as English, Jewish and Polish, and who was recognised by Rory as one of the Africans Neal was involved with at the time. Ascherson of Argyll, and of Islington and Warsaw, is like Lermontov, a Russian poet descended from some Scottish Learmonths, and like the Pole Conrad, who fell in love with the British Merchant Navy. This plasticity – this being like, this imagining yourself – is something that most people would say they were familiar with, and you don't have to be a wizard of the thing for it to suggest to others a movement of the spirit, a success, rather than the failure detected by policemen of the separate self. Neal is certainly his own man, utterly individual, with his own co-ordinating writer's art to call the shapes, and his own politics. I have got carried away.

Rory's picture of me is the tense treatment of a tense and self-righteous young man, very different from the weeper of the diaries. I am an enraged daffodil. It is like the picture of Dorian Gray – in seeming to take the frowns, ire and strain of the prig from Scotland wound up by the Downing anathemas, while relinquishing the lachrymose, but also amenable and conversible, other self.

In the playroom at Marchmont records rolled: Humphrey Lyttelton's 'Maryland, My Maryland', Leadbelly's blues. It was from Leadbelly records that Rory learnt to play the guitar, and to sing his folk songs and ballads, and repartees of his own composing. Nimble fingers took him into his intent pictures and into origami, fly-tying, guddling for trout: a Box of Delights, given to his mother, contained the fruits of his activities. Innocence had to make what it could of these delights, of these beautiful places, this privileged life. It certainly seemed, at times, outlandish. Here were boys who used to arrive for their holidays from Eton down their own single-track railway line. There was a chapel in the house where Muriel Spark's friend, Father Philip Caraman, would appear, like a crumpled cowslip, as from his priest's hole, to say Mass. Marse in the Merse . . . Here was a nest of Catholic gentlefolk, in touch with a literary sub-culture much preoccupied, in those days, with the convert's Catholic novel. I was no convert to any of that, and in other respects too, one of Marchmont's more exotic guests.

My love for Rory made light of all such difficulties. A Communist friend of mine from Scotland went on to me about how, when his train to Cambridge had stopped at York, he had been afflicted with the fearful sight of a tall young man in an Inverness cape and a Tam o' Shanter, clad in tartan trews, a brace of pheasants over his shoulder, and in his hand a guitar, from which trailed a sky-blue ribbon: surely there could be no such person as this who was actually Scottish. Apart from that afflicted observer, though, I can remember no one who minded Rory's dandyism. He was as kind as he was colourful and funny.

His art depended on a rapt attention to the natural world, which had been preceded by Alexander Hume's rapt attention, and indeed by that of the scientist Hugh Miller, in his hyper-observant autobiography; in a wholly undiminishing sense, it can be called a modest and an unromantic art. The directors of the art scene which he entered on leaving Cambridge were not drawn to such attentions, on the part of young painters, and would no doubt have been content to regard them as craft rather than art. He was to respond for a while, in his nimble and versatile way, to their expectations, and to new approaches, but he eventually returned to nature, to portraits of onions and other roots, of flowers and leaves withered and in bloom, and it was chiefly these, together with the early work, which in the end made his name.

His sister and his brother Robin, then a barrister in London, were also to become my friends, and when Robin and his wife Brigid moved to Marchmont, he leased me, for next to nothing, the nearby farmhouse of Polwarth Rhodes. He held patrician views which he liked to debate into the Border night with left-wing friends, and he was later to prove the least truckling or dissembling of Parliamentary candidates. In the course of an ill-fated political career he told a heckler in, as it were, Galashiels that the reason why the heckler's pension was smaller than that of a member of the judiciary was that the member of the judiciary was worth more.

'All good things must come to an end,' said my grandmother on occasion, and the McEwens were to meet with a series of harrowing misfortunes. Around 1980, Rory became ill with cancer. Robin, a brilliant, driven man, fell into a depression from which he found no escape. Two of their brothers also died, together with two of Robin's children. One of these children, Kate, an artist and strange spirit, who would start from the hedgerows round Polwarth with a kestrel on her shoulder, and sit down to supper with a snake in her jeans pocket, was discovered drowned in East Africa. By then, her father was gone, having befriended an owl, who would come to his garden to have its snow-white ruff paddled by the laird. The last time I saw the inside of Marchmont, young people from London, there for one of these funerals, creatures of the Sixties, some of them hippies, some of them strangers, drifted like ghosts through the darkened and deserted rooms.

Rory's illness lasted many months. I remember his sprightly letters from Australia, where he went to consult a doctor. Steroids buoyed him up at times, at the expense of a wild wish to help the world, which sent him to Clarence House to enlist the Queen Mother. At other times, having lost his hair to the steroids, he would sit calmly in his hospital bed, dressed in the white linens of an Indian trouser suit and in a turban planted with a costume jewel and surmounted by an aspiring feather. On one occasion, his watercolour paints and brushes lay by his bed; beside them, evoking the slow sessions of the past, the swift picture of a flower. Back into my mind, too, came a youthful drive with him into the depths of the English countryside to inspect a vicar's carnations.

He asked me to visit him at his house near mine in London, one Friday evening. He was dressed in a grey suit such as my Uncle Bob might have worn. He was about as sprightly as a judge, and indeed there were judgements, quiet ones, in what he had to say. He spoke quietly, and, as he always did, he listened carefully. He knew, I think, that this would be the last evening of his life.

CHAPTER TEN

Poor Man

I had discovered by now that the working class were not the only ones who read books. I had discovered what it was to be in the company of those whose families were well-off, and I was to go on to learn about a clearly-defined and yet miscellaneous London life engaged in by these people and by their lookalikes and soundalikes. It included the pompous and the laid-back, grandees and upstarts, the outrageous and the polite, stylish, bookish men and women in whom Bloomsbury survived, *Observer* correspondents, literary travellers in remote regions, attenders of parties, Patrick Leigh Fermor's prose style and romantic war, Ken Tynan's wit and Monsignor Gilbey's top hat. It included versions of the pair in *Brideshead Revisited*: the golden youth and his jumped-up intimate – Lord Marchmain's son Sebastian and the novelist's surrogate, plain Charles Ryder.

Looking at Mark Boxer's illustrations for Anthony Powell's novel sequence of the Fifties and Sixties, 'A Dance to the Music of Time', I have known myself to reflect that such images were once as far from me as any foreign country. Powell's books are a guide to the life to which I am referring, where there was always someone to be found boring, or to be called 'one of my oldest friends'; and the same is true, as I noticed in the Fifties, of Henry Green's novel *Loving* ('the last word on posh houses'). Another such guide can be found, in anticipatory form, in *Some People*, a judicious title, by the sapient Harold Nicolson, a visitor to Cambridge, in my time, who served as a role model for a section of the *jeunesse*; and *Some People* can also, I think, be considered a guide to Anthony Powell.

Published in 1927, this is a very amusing book in which Nicolson, a diplomat and an ambassador's son, semi-fictionalises his encounters with the great and the boring and sets out to rag them. There's a perfume of the hard to get and the hard to get to, of exotic objects and place-names: 'Sheikh Sa'ad and Magdalen, that Coromandel cabinet . . .' It rocks to the motion of the Orient Express. The first person singular is disclosed, though only intermittently, as a touch deficient. 'Considerations of high life assumed for him an importance which appeared, even to me, a little exaggerated,' says the narrator, snubbing himself in passing: but we hardly know where the snub is being directed when a silly fellow is seen talking to a 'buck nigger'.

The key encounter, from the present point of view, is with J. D. Marstock, a schoolfellow, a vacant sporting paragon, who is happened upon later at a kind of finishing-school in France, and elsewhere. Early in the Powell sequence, a finishing-school in France is featured, where the bore and future worldly success Widmerpool is happened upon by Nicholas Jenkins, the narrator, whose social sense can now and then be thought a little boring, even by the appreciative, and by the author too. Marstock is deficient as the Nicolson persona is deficient – only much more so. And Marstock is like Widmerpool.

These schoolfellows can at times be thought to belong to a fellowship of the more or less, the fiercely or faintly deficient. Favouritism confers its usual benefits on the author's principal representative, on the narrator in each case, whose interesting deficiency would seem to owe something to Proust's Marcel. In each case, nevertheless, the bore bears an affinity to the memorialist who rags him and who was at school with him – an affinity which commemorates that school. Both of these writers can on occasion write as if sealed in their shared background, in which schools matter, old friends and old bores matter, and deficiency lies in wait.

There is no former pupil like the former pupil of a public school: the nostalgia I have displayed for the Royal High is in a different league. Both in Anthony Powell's novels of the Thirties and in the retrospects of the decade embodied in the novels that followed, this impression of the hermetic is strikingly imparted by their preoccupation with the otherness of Jews. They are there as outsiders – exotic and at times dubious outsiders. In *Afternoon Men* a bore who doesn't seem to like Jews concedes:

'One can't dismiss whole races at a time.' The author of these absorbing and very funny books finds Jews strangely interesting; he doesn't want them dismissed, or, in Saki's expression, mislaid; a joke which terms dislike of monkeys 'anti-simianism' can hardly be termed gravely anti-semitic. And at least, you could say, they are there. Most categories of outsider are very dimly registered in these annals of school, university, the professions, high life, and the low life happened upon in the bohemia of Fitzroy Square. Readers who feel excluded by all this, however, may take heart. Such is authorship, such is human life, that even the enclosed – Nicolson, Waugh in his later fictions, and at moments Powell too – have wished to present themselves as outsiders. Nicolson was to become a Labour politician – as well as a man who was to worry, in 1930, that the Foreign Office might be 'flooded by clever Jews'.

This fascination with Jewish people solicits me because of my own fascination with them. The otherness of Jews was a feature of my first world; they then became an abiding sympathy, and more. I began to think about what had been done to them at about the age when I learnt that some of it had been done to the people of the Scottish Highlands, and it was to remain with me, as with many, in times when philosemitism grew to be a custom of the literary culture, and in later times too, when philosemites could feel obliged to oppose the policies of Israeli governments. I regard the Holocaust film *Shoah* as one of the most important of the modern world's works of art, and Primo Levi as one of its most important writers. The post-war hope that genocidal projects might never occur again has meanwhile become virtually inconceivable.

Before long, I was to see less of this upper-class life, and then very little of it. For one thing, I became interested once more in football. Playing it and watching it helped to wean me from the romantic game of alienation and distress which I had played during my adolescence, and which had given me a taste for exotic and patrician scenes. My earliest football memory is of a twilight of low-lying coal-black rain-clouds and of stumbling across a morass of a pitch which some bold spirit seems to have been trying to bring under the plough. Near hand are the clangs and glows of the village smithy, where horseshoes are sent sizzling and reeking into hooves. Down a path, the further drama and illumination of the football field. I belong to a nebula of urchins tugged about by the blazing star on the ball.

The pitch was that of the local team, the Gilmerton Drumbirds (so-called after the Adam country house at the edge of the village, the Drum, of which none of us was otherwise aware). They wore jerseys of black and white vertical stripes. Their coach was a sterling character named Baxter, centre-half of the professional side in Edinburgh, Hibernian. The blazing star was Bailie Hutchison, a slip of a boy with a chestnut scalp-lock, whose skill was dribbling and whose game was to do it all the time. There have often been Hutchisons in Scottish football. Gordon Smith of Hibernian was just such a virtuoso.

I had played the game on such pitches – and in the streets at Moredun, delivering wireless commentaries the while. In later years I had been keen to gather that my father's father had played for Rangers, and my Kirkcaldy uncle had played as a schoolboy for Scotland. It was in my blood, I decided. This did not enable me to play well. But it caused me to take the game up, somewhat to my surprise, when I left Cambridge. I was a lesser light, and sometimes a darkness, in the small team I played for. This could be galling, but it also seemed part of the whole idea. I was now and then to think that by playing football I was rejoining the working class, diverging from the road that led, for romantic scholarship boys, to a point above their station, and I was always pleased to hear, from the fastidious, about the violent lowness of this grotesque enthusiasm.

It was a belief of the adolescence I imagined for myself that the spirit was willing but the flesh weak. I knew what my daughter was talking about when she said as a very small girl: 'I'm not a kisser. I'm a fighter.' But I was a fighter who had failed to fight his corner in the playground. I did not appear to have the strength for it. So, when I took up playing again, I reviewed my physical attributes, wondering whether I was suffi-ciently removed from the noodle to be up to these exertions.

According to my friend Jimmy Nichol, who played international rugby, my legs were all right: but they didn't move very fast. My upper-body strength was suspect, if not measly, according to doctors who had examined me. There was that stalk neck, those skinny arms, that fear of heading heavy balls that fell on you from dizzy heights. The left of me, moreover, was a lot less healthy than the right. The two sides of my person failed to agree. They were like my father and mother.

'He done great to get there,' said a professional player once, of one of his peers. I didn't often get there, and at worst it could all seem very like the time when I ran into an Irish garden and took a flying kick at a ball which proved to be a nautical mine, moored there for ornament. It was said of me that I was 'marvellously slow', and I was told at a reunion that I had all the qualities except speed and heart. I didn't mind the tussles, in fact, and I enjoyed the exhaustions; all-out physical effort was a boon, after the thousands of books by which I'd been immobilised. I can't remember a time when I felt physically well: but on the field I forgot to feel ill. Scanning the team's end-of-season record in 1961, I notice that I was credited with six goals. Some scribal error must be suspected here. My sporting career is exactly commemorated in the inscription on a far from ostentatious silver goblet, which dispenses with any mention of feats or honours and simply says: 'Karl Miller, footballer'.

The team was known as Battersea Park, after the place where we played. Some of us were actors, journalists, publishers, civil servants. There were fewer members of the proletariat than may have existed in my imagination of the enterprise. There were those who were morbidly anxious to score, and to be virtuosos; there was apt to be some confusion; but you did not go in fear of being dropped if you did not do great. The moving spirit was Tony White, who was afterwards to share the running of the side with the soccer journalist John Moynihan, a silent man with a matrimonial dedication to the game, and the air, in due course, of a sheriff from the badlands of the Rio Grande. I remember leaving the field at Battersea, alone, one winter Sunday afternoon. A mist had come down. There on the touchline, in horn-rims and flat cap, was the only other figure in sight – the Irish poet and misanthrope, Patrick Kavanagh, who seemed to have come to see a literary editor's feet of clay. Feet? I was covered in it. I lurched towards those cold eyes.

Tony was big and strong and eager, for ever being cut and gashed. He was the bloody man in the Shakespeare play. His rich dark eyes, boundless generosity and zest, and his lavish brush-strokes on the field of play, held us together. He was half-French, and had been at Downing. During his time at Cambridge he had been, in point of style, one of the dangerous new belt-buckle youth, and a very good romantic actor, who gave all of his honesty and sweet nature to Cyrano and Berowne. I was always to remember what he made, in his college-garden *Love's Labour's Lost*, of the final pledge to plainness of speech, Ber-owne's goodbye to 'taffeta phrases': 'By this white glove – how white the hand God knows . . .' The Rank Organisation thought of him as a possible star, and he might well have made one, of the independent, loner sort, in the days when Brando was setting his example. But he gave that up, and settled for being a lamplighter, and then a footballer and a freelance writer, who assisted with the memoirs of Alfie Hinds, the great escaper from prison, whose two sons played in the team. My own son Sam was later to do so too.

Battersea Park, Hyde Park, Wormwood Scrubs, Hackney Marshes, a village in Essex – these were our venues, and we would also go on foreign tours. Once upon a time we went to Mayo, where the locals were to be offended to read in an English paper an ironic reference, by one of our number, to 'muddied oafs'. The locals were not to know that Battersea liked the idea of muddied oafs. We sailed to Dieppe to play a team with professionals in it, running out in front of what we weren't used to, a crowd. Our captain, Tony, tripped over a sod and measured his length. Afterwards he offered up an elegant speech of thanks in the town hall. Our opponents, said a French paper, had been braced to meet *l'engagement physique, l'endurance et le style britannique*. Another French paper reported that their English cousins had appeared tired from the voyage.

There was a strange trip to Portugal. We drove out of Sloane Square in a van, leaving 'London a little lonelier tonight'. We lost a player on the way, having already lost a goalkeeper to the London suburbs, where his wife had broken out against his Easter defection in terms which had silenced the van. We descended through the beautiful pristine landscapes of Europe, with not a suburb or a factory to be seen, over various sierras and down into a countryside where Shakespearian banks of wildflowers bordered the winding roads. The destination was a semi-derelict mining town, where a Third Division side awaited our Britannic style. We sat by the chalets of a company village, looking up at a skyline crossed, every so often, by a sombrero'd cowboy on his mule. Presently, charismatic Peter Doherty, wit, actor and cowboy decorator, as the sour saying goes, lay spread-eagled naked on a hillside, being oiled for the combat. Later that night, wives and girlfriends of the team sprang naked into the firelight on the hill to perform a dance of reproof, aimed at the male bonding of their companions; several Iron Johns were abashed, or embarrassed. A girl who had come along with us for something to do, and who abstained from the dance of the indignant streakers, was later to marry Georgi Markov, the writer who was stabbed to death in London with the poisoned tip of an umbrella, at the order of the President of his native Bulgaria.

I played very badly in Portugal, perched on a new pair of boots, and I had a low moment in my chalet, telling myself that the team would be less bizarre if these new boots were hung up. One or two of the players, I ought to make clear, were really good: Malcolm and Eddie Southan, for instance, and Peter Doherty. Peter's trip to Portugal enthralled his mates, both on and off the field. The last scene of the tour was played out in the village square, where a lovely maiden stepped forward in spectacular nuptial finery, under the impression that Peter had pledged himself. It was all we could do to get away in the van.

In 1976, Tony broke a leg on the field, was struck by an embolism and died. This, you could say, was love's labours lost, and the loss of Tony is still mourned by his friends, who still write poems about him. There would have been no explaining the matter to those who felt that the loss was occasioned by a trivial pursuit. Football was part of his move to do what he wanted to do, and to stay clear of the ambitions for which his background had prepared him and which had engrossed many of the people he knew at school and university.

I learnt a lot about football from Danny Blanchflower of Spurs, who wrote about it in the *New Statesman* when I was literary editor there, and from the musician Hans Keller, who wrote about it for me when I edited the *Listener*, and whose discussions of the Brazilian sides of 1970 and before are among the best pieces of criticism, on any subject, that I have come across. For Keller, these sides were made up of intelligent and imaginative individuals who belonged to an intelligent and imaginative team. He taught the lessons of their mastery, and used them to bombard *le style britannique*. Both were obstinate men, talkers, teases. Danny's words were often cryptic and poetic: but they could also be as effective as his performance on the field, with his awkward elbowy action and priceless forward lobs from midfield. He was held to be slow, but was lightning, Battersea found, when he saw someone dwelling on the ball and looking about in the manner of the shrewd midfielder. I used to go with him to his games, home and away. One Saturday at six in the evening, on a platform at Ipswich Station, a frieze of Spurs people became one of my souvenirs. On his own stood the manager, Bill Nicholson, no relation to Harold, an unweening senior citizen, twice as taciturn as John Moynihan. At a distance stood the team, among them the rock Dave Mackay, formerly of Newtongrange Star in Midlothian, and among them the words of the captain, Blanchflower. He and Nicholson were a union of opposites which worked very well: their team was the first to do 'the double' and achieve victory in both the League and the Cup competitions.

The tedium of star sport, of winning teams and winning nations, the tedium of points and results and averages, is easily decried. But it would be daft to pretend that the beauties of the game aren't more conspicuous on its great occasions than they are among exponents of Sunday football, poor man's football. Football is like dance, and it can be experienced as a kind of music; and its dramatic interest is undeniable. Its beauties derive from human qualities which are, for the most part, no less evident in the arts: skill, guile, grace, presence of mind, depth of purpose, courage and aggression. Force, flair and order, one might say for short, if it didn't make one sound like Mussolini. And it depends for its appreciation – much in the way that literature may appear to do in requiring the sense of an author – on an ability to distinguish person from pattern, the dancer from the dance, the player from the play.

As a watcher, I have always been interested in players, quite a few of them foreigners in the English League, whose talents are disparaged or underrated by journalists and managers. The Frenchman Eric Cantona is a case in point. We have been told about this 'maverick's' mistakes, tricks and *tours de force*. Had he the 'character and intelligence' to adapt to English football? He scored three goals in the opening game of the 1992–3 season, the Charity Shield match, and it was then said of him by his manager at Leeds that he was still learning, learning to work hard, and that he would have to learn to score ugly goals as well as beautiful ones. He had none the less been vital to their capture of the League Championship. Less than half-way through the new season, his first full English season, he was sold, with his foreigner's bad habits, to Manchester United, who have now become the new League Champions.

Peter Beardsley and the Dane Jan Molby are players of this kind. Small, hunched Beardsley is a creator, rather than a powerful interferer with play, though he has scored his share of beautiful, thrifty goals. Liverpool sold him, to its detriment, while he was still in mid-talent, though getting on in years. Liverpool have also been willing to sell, and to drop, their playmaker, Molby. Burly, portly, slow, slightly sinister, he goes about the field rolling his passes, hardly breaking sweat, as if there was no speaking to him, though he speaks fluent Liverpool, and as if he has yet to learn to smile. He will be removed from the team while he can still do what he has been doing, just as Gordon Strachan was sold by Manchester United, in his old age, to Leeds, whom he helped to raise to the top of the table.

Gifted players can sometimes seem to be feared and disliked by the managements they are meant to secure, with Scottish bosses in the English League well to the phobic fore. Gifted players are never as 'inconsistent' and 'unpredictable' as authorities allege, and it wouldn't matter very much if they were: I dedicate this proposition to Blackburn's foreigner Roy Wegerle, a 'Roy of the Rovers' who has recently been sold – having been sent there often enough in the past – to Coventry. It is difficult to account for their treatment without reference to such fears, and without reference to a narrow-minded provincialism, and to the Keller hypothesis of a national style which enshrines hard work and physical commitment. One of the beauties of the game is that these qualities, desirable as they are, seldom win tournaments at the highest level, as the success of Brazil, Italy and Holland goes to show. Professional players can be heard to say that they want to express themselves on the park, and many managers seem reluctant to hear it. Self-expression and team effort are enemies: but they are also functions of one another, and, as such, among the life-giving dualities I like to think about. In football, as in literature, beauty, with its mysterious debt to self-expression, is functional, and very few teams have ever done well by piling up the ugly goals.

After the 1990 World Cup, I published an article claiming that Paul Gascoigne, then of Spurs, had been subjected to the treatment I have been describing. His experience of put-downs and blame followed a childhood marked by isolation and disruption, and his restlessness, mischief and comic turns, the unfurling at opponents of a brogue-obliterating tongue, may well have something to do with this. His talent is of the kind that suggests impairment to some; his restlessness has even received a suggestive freelance medical diagnosis. Elsewhere, his originally aphasic television interviews, mocked by journalists, have been linked to a previous speech defect. The article became a rhapsody of praise for his speaking football, which was quoted in the Spurs match programme – for a laugh over its long words. During the World Cup, 'he was a highly-charged spectacle on the field of play: fierce and comic, formidable and vulnerable, urchin-like and waif-like, a strong head and torso with comparatively frail-looking breakable legs, strange-eyed, pink-faced, fair-haired, tense and upright, a priapic monolith in the Mediterranean sun – a marvellous equivocal sight.'

Some months later, straining to do well in a domestic game, he risked that breakable leg and damaged a knee, and was told off in the newspapers for that, for the character deficiency which had driven him over the top. The injury was one from which there can be no certainty that he will recover in full. It would be a pity if the subtlety and dynamism of his game were to be lost this early in his career, and we were to be left to the aftermath of a horrible journalistic obsession, with its equal parts – well-known by now to the Royal Family – of adulation and spite.

He is, in his equivocal way, very close to the heart of a football culture which is both far-flung and intensely local. It contains the North-East of England, from which Gascoigne hails, together with the nearby Border country – regions which supplied the bandit reivers of the past and which have supplied several of the outstanding footballers of the modern world, some of whom bear the same names. It contains Battersea Park and Newtongrange Star, as well as Tottenham Hotspur. And it contains the Himalayan stadium, in Ladakh, where a commentator's lament for an unfortunate goalkeeper was broadcast on the tannoy: 'Alas, alas, all signs of life have disappeared from Chang's kicks as the shadows of evening descend over our pitch.' I seem to remember Chang from his days at Battersea.

Values and valuations are no more stable in literature than they are in football, and the pains and frustrations are just as acute. I was to go on to spend my time as a student of these and other aspects of writing, and as a seeker of writers to support, among them, as it turned out, V. S. Naipaul, Dan Jacobson, Kingsley Amis and Philip Larkin, Seamus Heaney and Michael Hofmann. There were causes, too, which I was keen to support, and I only wish I had made a better job of it. Few of the pieces I published when I was first an editor gave me more satisfaction than one in the *Spectator* by Richard Wollheim, entitled 'The Road to Toleration', which came out at the time when the case was being pressed, in the end successfully, for removing homosexuality from the ambit of the criminal law. I always wanted to be an editor, and I have been one for forty years. Latterly I have taught literature at University College London, while founding and editing the *London Review of Books*, of which I later became a co-editor. I have done what I wanted to do, though I would have liked to be more of a writer of books than I have succeeded in being. Save for that, I can count myself lucky in my working life.

The end of my time at the *London Review*, which came about in the autumn of 1992, coincided with this last chapter of the present book. Some of the immediate circumstances of my departure were written in the stars, and read there by the *Evening Standard* astrologer, Patric Walker, who forecast the following, for Leos, on the Monday of the week in question: 'Take the fullest possible advantage of challenging aspects over the next couple of days or so to air your opinions and grievances. You may dislike having to be so forthright and forceful over a career or professional matter.' On the Tuesday I was due to publish, and did publish, a piece in the *Guardian* which spoke of my departure: 'My connection with the paper dates back to its kick-start in 1979, but I have never shared, or wished to share, in its ownership. My co-editor and I have worked together in these capacities for the last five years, but in recent times we have had difficulty in doing so. In the circumstances, it eventually seemed to me a good idea that I should leave, not so much retiring as resigning.'

I had wanted to speak for myself, 'forthrightly', in anticipation of what might be said by others. But misgivings arrived when I looked at the piece on the page, and at the accompanying photograph, which made my flesh crawl with its air of a man about to murder somebody. I felt that there was generally a great deal to be said for saying nothing. I felt that the article registered as a plea, an exercise in self-pity, which was also a ploy. Ends met. First person and last shook hands. I was back with the paradox of the weeping assassin, with the complaining part of me which began to think about taking early retirement at the age of sixteen, but which was to hang on in the world, and to glare at it. The comedy, it seemed, was not yet finished.

I am sure it was right for me to leave, and I'd had enough practice at this sort of thing to be prepared for what happens when you stop doing what you have been doing, with a will, for a long time. What happened this time, however, has been worse, and grief is the only name for it that I can think of. It is among the experiences in this book which I have exposed with a shyness trenching on horror, in the belief that the book would lose its meaning if it were withheld. When I received a letter from Neal Ascherson saying, in German, that a light had gone out, his valediction caused me to feel that I wanted to go on editing for a bit longer, while knowing that the latest of my journalistic exits is likely to be my last. It made me feel like Drummond's prematurely-buried fiancée.

Some three and a half decades before this, I spent two years as a research student, the first of them at Cambridge and the second on a fellowship at Harvard. I was trying to get into the Scottish literary culture of the late eighteenth and early nineteenth centuries, in order to examine what I thought of as 'puritanism' – the Jeanie Deans antithesis of the liberation ethic of my own lifetime. Many years later I wrote a book on the period, my Cockburn book. So I must have been interested. But my first year of graduate studies proved languorous and unproductive. Perhaps I was tired of all this education. At all events, I developed a horror of the Cambridge University Library catalogues and preferred the stupor induced by my gas fire. I did not wish to enlist in 'the common pursuit of true judgement', if this was to mean contributions, and conscientious objections, to Leavis's war with the metropolis. I'd had enough of judgement – but not of truth. I still have some hopes there, which were to survive its deconstruction in America, where the formation of an institutionalised orthodoxy hostile to such hopes could be seen, by ambitious academics, to have driven Leavis's judgemental literary criticism into the disgraceful past. This truth of mine, I should add, is nothing like the one laid up in heaven for some form of eventual full disclosure. I can't imagine it purged of uncertainty and invention.

Eisenhower's America, though, woke me up. It was a land of promise then for the left-wing young who visited it from Britain, who forgot to disapprove of its politics, and were able to invent for themselves a romantic new world and a refuge from a class-ridden society. The highly professionalised academic scene was admirable and imposing and a little depressing, I found, so far as its attentions to literature were concerned. In flight from the sufferings and treacheries of his war years, Paul de Man was shortly to deny to a Harvard professor that he had collaborated with the Nazis, to proceed to a position of authority in the same competitive institutional milieu, and to assist in the conversion of some part of it to the new orthodoxy of Deconstruction – which has now, in its turn, departed from the scene, or been radically transformed. At Harvard I made friends with Richard Poirier and Daniel Aaron, and the tonic Mary McCarthy, whose books – together with the novels of Bellow and Malamud and the poems of Robert Frost and Robert Lowell – were to teach me an American lesson, and to help to steer the course of my post-adolescent literary taste. I used to go down to Staten Island for stays with Marius Bewley, Late Victorian dandy literatus and Jamesian Anglophile. Marius was an excellent critic and historian who had worked with Leavis and was fond of him, but about whom George Barker had been misled. Rigor Leavis had not set in.

I got married in Cambridge, Massachusetts, to Jane Collet, English, Scottish and Jewish – a wearer of Rebecca's vest, among other garments, though she would not want it put that way – whom I had come to know during my later years at the other Cambridge, and we drove round America in a Buick – easy riders, in the romantic style that was taking hold there – with Rory McEwen and a brother. Marriage was to change my life. The self-devotion which I have been writing about in this book was exposed to the making of a home and the raising of three children. 'Settle down?' said my father in mid-life: 'I doubt if I could do that any more.' Well, he had never done it, and now I had. The narrator of Ian McEwan's novel *The Black Dogs* offers a remark which I trust is not intended as the error of an unreliable narrator: this narrator says he should have learnt that 'the simplest way of restoring a lost parent was to become one yourself; that to succour the abandoned child within, there was no better way than having children of your own to love.' Plangent, but for many people, I would have thought, fair enough.

The old orphan attitudes – he who is kept out tries both to stay out and to get in – shrank back at the blaze of a hearth. But they were not to go for good. They have helped to write this book, and they have troubled my marriage. To be married at a time when principles of independence gained ground was to discover that a relationship which has always been difficult for some could become more difficult than before. I haven't, however, recoiled from these painful principles. I hardly know where I would have been without them. I am glad that my wife has been able to pursue a working life of her own, and I admire what she has done as a teacher in schools and universities and as a feminist writer. Another way of expressing some of this would be to say that my youth has remained with me, as youths do, but that the regard for marriage which came with a new sense of the claims on my mind of people other than myself has remained with me too.

We returned from America to a Britain soon to be patriotically stirred by the Government's Suez plot. With the exception of the *Observer*, newspapers were, as so often, well able to see the point of waging war. Those readers who had missed the point were sufficient to form a capacity crowd in Whitehall, and I stood in Downing Street with some Girton graduates, calling out in their sopranos that 'Eden must go.' I was now to be in government myself, in a small and ephemeral way. I spent a year in the suit of an assistant principal at the Treasury. Among its new young men was Robert Armstrong, who was subsequently, in Australia, with reference to an official pronouncement, to coin the phrase 'economical with the truth', in a bid to save his government's face by suppressing the *Spycatcher* charges of Communist subversion. Suez had already made clear that British governments could be economical with the truth to the point of outright denial (and there were quite a few Cambridge graduates who already suspected, at this early stage, that subversive Anthony Blunt had been economical with it). One of my senior civil servants was later to say at a memorial service that 'truth was something not to be tampered with': I am sure he meant it, and I wonder what he can have made of his masters at the time of the Suez collusion.

The civil servants I worked with were at least as able as the job description and corporate image required them to be. They were scrupulous, unpretentious people, rather less hierarchical in outlook than their military equivalents, though there was plenty of talk, among juniors, of promotion. I remember an occasion when juniors were stood in a corridor of power to listen to Harold Macmillan – one of the ministers responsible for Suez – praise, in a very hollow fashion, the 'integretah' of civil servants. But it did not occur to me that the compliment was undeserved. There was talk of corruption, out there somewhere in the country at large, and we had an official who would lift to a nostril some file in which evidence was felt to reside. But I would have thought that corruption of any sort was quite uncommon in the central government of the Fifties, for all the pressures that politicians, among others, have shown themselves capable of applying. I formed a sneaking affection for a senior known as Pike-Lees, whom I was never to meet. His real name, apparently, was Pickles.

The next year was spent at Shepherd's Bush, as a producer on BBC Television's *Tonight*, a current affairs programme later seen as a pioneering instance of the demotic, democratic, investigative, pleasurable BBC fostered by Hugh Greene, a far better BBC than the one there is now; and then on an old-style admiring arts programme by the name of *Monitor*, powered by the hwyl of Huw Wheldon, its presenter, a kind of British Army Welsh wizard, destined to become Controller of BBC Television.

A brisk-to-hysterical place, BBC Television then, where studio directors were compared to fighter pilots, and a trainee could be told by a producer: 'You're either a genius or you're not. And I haven't got time to find out.' Broadcasting didn't seem to suit me any more, if it had ever suited me, and I was relieved to be offered Robert Kee's job as literary editor of the *Spectator*, having sat at Kee's knee in the capacity of reviewer. Off I went to Bloomsbury and the dear old printed word.

The London literary world was more complex than Leavis made out. Log-rolling cliques there certainly were: but they were usually at odds with one another, and no single group could be thought to be in control of the reputation and reception of writers. All there was of that kind of thing was an amorphous upper-class presence given over to a resentment of upstarts and of the unfamiliar. At parties and long lunches journalists and publishers met, as they do still, to gossip about the book trade. Literary editors scanned the lists of over-producing publishers, as they still do, in search of stories and of a content for their journals and for the book pages of newspapers. But the disparity between the scale and scope of publishers' output and the response to that which journalism is prepared to offer has increased with the years, and with the demise of journals and the abbreviation of book pages. Publishers have turned for coverage to television, where, as they may not have perceived, books are at present extremely unpopular. Those 'tile-shaped objects' – as Alan Pryce-Jones used to call them, when communicating to literary aspirants the need to produce one at the first possible opportunity – have more or less fled the screen.

Authors were important then, and would continue to be, for all the rise of theories alleging their unimportance. People like them, after all. My early excitements on the subject are meant to suggest this, to suggest, for instance, that poor lonely people like the poor lonely people who write books and want to be liked for it. Such excitements go very far back in time, of course. In the 1850s Hugh Miller wrote in his autobiography of the occasion when, as a boy in Cromarty, away there at the very tip of things, he saw for the first time 'a human creature . . . that

had actually published a book. Poor Miss Bond was a kindly
sort of person . . .' She was also, Miller writes, like the original
of Jeanie Deans, a 'proud bodie'. 'Miss Bond the authoress'
never came through with the patronage she had seemed about to
provide, but she was not forgotten.

'The authoress put them there,' said a cowboy decorator once
of a vase of flowers on a table. I liked the sound of that. It
seemed to me to convey that authoresses and authors had put
something on the table which made all the difference to people's
lives. There were those who wanted books, wanted authors, and
wanted to find them in the books they read. Will the table be
bare in another forty years' time? The literary scene is shivering
now in the mid-winter of a long recession, which belongs to a
savage and desperate contemporary world. Authorship has survived such disorders in the past, and it's reasonable to think that
there will be writers in the new century, and that there will be
leading writers too, of whom so much has been made. In the
Fifties and thereafter, to a degree which it has been right to
question, and which you do not need to be a theorist to
question, leading writers dominated the scene.

The literary scene has perhaps grown dirtier, but then it has
never been very clean. Jealousy and hostility have always been
aspects of authorship, and of what it has to fear. I couldn't fail
to notice, when I started editing, that, for many writers, all
times are hard times. There are those who write out of anxiety
and self-pity, out of one or other of the available orphanings, in
a world of enemies and of rivals. And they are all of them
exposed to the chances and tender mercies of journalism and
publishing, and of a sometimes unreachable public; their rejec-
tion by constructors of great traditions, and by deconstructors
of authorship, can hardly have disturbed them as much – a
minor pain for the minor writer, so to speak. Meanwhile, from
the standpoint of journalism, it can be tempting to think of a
free-for-all in which war and peace, levity and earnest, entertainment and instruction, politics and letters, shade into one another,
and in which the reputations of particular writers serve both as
armament and as target – with friendly forces not that fond of

each other, dealers in sentiment and fine feelings rarely sentimental. It is tempting to come out with such descriptions, but there is too much anger in them. A sweeter view of the same scene, with a stress on sympathy and probity, and indeed on the exercise of judgement, is also possible, and I have known what it was to hold it.

In the light, or half-light, of the foregoing descriptions I have no difficulty in imagining how the present book will be discussed. Auberon Waugh, a rival editor over the years, will take time to discuss it, and what he will say can be inferred from a newspaper article of 1991, which noted that he'd 'routinely upbraided' me as 'a suitable receptacle for dried excrement, as the person Waugh most despises'. I am his bore – a school bore who also happens to be one of those workers he dislikes. The article made me think what playing football made me think. It restored me to the kind of people with whom I grew up, and who are routinely abused by Waugh – an outcome which would have been, in some sort, part of what he intended in speaking of his antipathy. He writes, I feel, out of the sense of exclusion which some writers display, and which causes him to wish to be seen as upper-class. It is just as easy to see him as an orphan, with a celebrated freezing father.

When I entered the house in Gower Street where the *Spectator* was lodged, two of the sharpest tongues in the business were attacking their tall typewriters after a long lunch. The three of us were parked like survivors in what appeared to be a tarpaulined World War Two fuselage, crashed in the back garden. It was as if we would end up eating each other. Bernard Levin and Alan Brien were respectively the Westminster Correspondent and the theatre critic. Neither of them was as menacing as their invectives, and many of these were, as they say, in fun. Bernard shared his cubicle in the fuselage with my friend Rory, the paper's cartoonist, who around this time, in a racecourse tent, threw a potato at the Attorney-General, Sir Reginald Manningham-Buller – Bernard's Sir Reginald Bullying-Manner. You'd think Bernard would have been pleased. Instead, he whirled an umbrella, on the grounds that Rory should settle down and make the best of himself: 'You have thrown your potato of talent at the Attorney-General of life – and missed.'

The journal's proprietor was Ian Gilmour of Craigmillar Castle, who also edited it for a while, and it was very lively – Tory radical in tendency, with rushes of Labour blood. Ian had at earlier moments seemed to be on the brink of declaring for Labour, but can hardly have been wooed to the plunge by an abrasive lawsuit in which Labour leaders, including Dick Crossman, successfully sued when the paper reported that they had astonished the natives of Italy by their consumption of whisky at a conference – a grave charge, in those days. This success, Ian devoutly and correctly held, had been dubiously earned. When I joined the paper, it was one in which veteran belletrists could be read, some of them with profit, where a more than geographical Bloomsbury connection remained, and where pieces were carried which instructed you in how to see trespassers off your land. But new notes were being struck too. The Movement school owed a portion of its origin to the paper, and I wanted there to be more of that. There was a line from Gower Street to the Gower Peninsula, where Kingsley Amis's Welsh phase was proceeding.

Romanticism, Modernism, the Movement – there are different orders of magnitude and of solemnity here. But the Movement was to warrant a place in literary history. It came to me as a change from the orphan attitudes, the dissident individualism, embodied in the symbiotic other two, as they were now to appear. I persuaded myself that it had salutary things to say about the self-devotion which is inalienably present in literature, but to which, as I was by now more aware, literature has its own challenges to offer. It promised an escape from the darkly suffering major or momentous writer. The Movement was rational and in a sense civic. It was as comic and democratic as the new BBC. The xenophobic strain I did not take very seriously; I was in tune with the exception that was made, by some of them, for America; and I was inclined to condone, in some of them, their streak of cruelty. Like many other streaks of cruelty, this was often visited on foreigners and – once or twice, after the dispersal of the group – on Jews.

Here were the writings of distressed bachelors, who went on to furnish an account – Kingsley Amis's in the main – of marriage, of the woes there are in that too. As a recently married man myself, I responded to these concerns, and was to form, and to retain, the view that Amis's comedies are a splendid achievement. Both Amis and Philip Larkin were widely regarded, at this stage, as teddy-boy profaners of literature. 'We disposed of Kingsley Amis (vulgar, dull and squalid)': the disposers here were Ivy Compton-Burnett and Elizabeth Taylor, novelists whom Amis has admired. The sentence, with its spade and dark lantern, has been attributed in print to the year 1955 and to the second of these two writers. She meant, I think, to attribute its sentiment to the first, to Ivy alone, and it was the sort of thing that was always being said by elders and betters. Then came a taste, mostly male, for Movement descriptions of an English scene. 'Exactly the chap's sort of thing': what Amis once said of James Bond's classy appurtenances might have been said of his own early books, as taken-to by their early readers. Movement descriptions were thought both comical and empirical – 'empirically true', as Larkin says of the snapshot of a lady. These were features which a chap could also find in other books of the day, and I was able to find them, when V. S. Naipaul brought out his *House for Mr Biswas*, in its masterly account of a West Indian scene. In time, Larkin was to be recognised as a poet of rare distinction, and there were also to be those for whom he was an English patriot. Before the very eyes of the readership which had seen them as friends of the people, both he and Amis were to reveal themselves as right-wing. Arise, Sir Kingsley.

For much of the present century the popularity of poetry has been on the wane: and yet the authority of poets has, in certain contexts, mattered more than that of other sorts of writer. It was to poets of the time, rather than to novelists, that critics turned for living proof of what they were urging, and, to a degree that now seems antique, these poets were willing to be critics. Eliot was at this time the leading authority of the kind, and of the others Robert Graves and William Empson were particularly attractive to Movement people. 'Making the difficult look easy,' wrote Ronald Bottrall in a poem in Empson's praise. Empson could also make it look difficult: but it was never in doubt that, as I was to hear him say late in life, he had wanted to try to help to get things clear. I was unable to feel the same about the precepts of, for example, Auden. My availability to precept had, in fact, receded, and would continue to recede with the onset of a preoccupation with the dual and the doubtful and the diverse – a preoccupation displayed and illuminated, in their different ways, by my next-door neighbour from the deep past, William Drummond, and by William Empson.

Precept was an instrument which the Movement employed with some skill. But even during my spell as a subaltern Movementeer, I felt like a rest from it – with its one thing rather than another where it was possible to want both, and to discover both in the one thing. It was possible to want both sound and sense, ornament and austerity, and not to want to be confined to the one apparatus of critical terms, with a name that began with a capital letter. The terms 'Classical' and 'Romantic' were known for their imperfections, and for the imperfections of the opposi-tional thinking to be found among preceptors who saw them-selves as standing on one side or the other of the divide. Those were terms, nevertheless, of which, in their imperfect, renovated senses, lots of people, including myself, still felt that they needed to make use.

Having given myself to *The Waste Land* one adolescent after-noon – advisedly unfazed by all incomprehensions – I had for several years read Eliot's poems with great interest – an interest constrained, though, and rendered somewhat uncritical, by a consciousness of his worth. But I couldn't take the politics of his religion, or the drawing-room martyrdoms of his later plays, which finally expired in the West End by the light of his impresario's cigar. In the Fifties, on almost all sides, he was revered and obeyed; even the Movement, which disliked so much and so many, withheld its question. Corporals would return from National Service hoping to put on incorruption and intending to join the nearest high church. He was a saint. He was severe. He was a major poet. And he had worked in a bank and was now a publisher. He wore a suit. Those were the days when poets wore suits and did mundane respectable jobs. Socialists and agnostics took part in the worship, and so did his critics, who were eager to comply with a set of principles which rested on the premise of a saving spiritual superiority – Eliot's and theirs – and of an escape from emotion, and which also rested on an admiration for royal families and for certain nations and traditions at the expense of others. With some disregard for the history of civilisation, this was called Classical.

You could not hope to call yourself Classical if you were in the habit of hurrying from a Glasgow close on a Saturday afternoon dressed in a jersey and bound in your spots and carbuncles for the football; the difference in religion between the Celtic and the Rangers support would have been quite immaterial. Over in Morningside Edinburgh, however, John Gray, whose game was golf and who hurried off to the Royal and Ancient course at St Andrews, would in his time have qualified for the description. He was a Catholic convert who had converted from Romanticism, abandoning a poetry in which intonations of Laforgue and hints of the impending Eliot have been caught. Herbert Grierson once spoke of the 'French feathers' he'd detected in the poetry of Wilde: perhaps one might say that John Gray's French feathers were transferred to Eliot's cap – on the royal road to Classicism. Late in life he tried his hand at verse in which a dry manner of the early Eliot was revived, as if by a member of the club. Gray was a joiner of clubs.

The obstinate importance of poetry in times when it was supposed to have been forgotten is the more remarkable for what could sometimes seem to be the woebegone human indifference of two of the most important poets to practise in Britain in the course of the present century. Eliot's verse was to convey that human life is grim and sordid, and not what it was, with a nadir apparent in the behaviour of the clerk and typist who 'couple like bugs' in the ambience of his early poetry; and it conveys – though with nothing like the old unction – that our hope must lie in being eligible for a better world. Those who felt they could deal with the first of these messages were not always comfortable with the second, and salvation was before very long to reach the end of its heyday. When the biographies began, however, the imperatives of salvation were by and large respectfully treated. Of the modern miserable whose sufferings were mainly dispelled by his second marriage, and of the friendships with two women which preceded that marriage, Lyndall Gordon writes in complicit fashion, summoning up a justified sinner, though without making light of what happened here, in the human world: 'His passion for immortality was so commanding that it allowed him to reject each of these women with a firmness which shattered their lives.'

The other misery is Larkin. He, too, wore a suit and did a job. 'Of course I know who you are,' Empson is reputed to have said to him, in a university lavatory. 'You're the man who's come to help us with the library.' His standing as a poet was to grow to a point where it could seem beyond question. A triumph for the plain style, I thought, as others did – though his style is not as plain as all that: it was somehow satisfying that his old friend and confederate, Amis, should latterly have raised a Movement objection to the touches of taffeta that came of his propensity for the eloquent close – for arrows in the air, the intense inane of infinite blue skies. In the midst of this triumph, he got married to Margaret Thatcher. As with Eliot, those on the left who had welcomed his poems swallowed their regrets, or failed to feel any, in the face of his politicisation. As for his own regrets – at the absence of love and then the imminence of death – these had always been freely expressed in his poems.

By the Humber, Larkin complained every bit as much as Drummond did by the Esk. When I first read Eliot, and then Larkin, I don't think I asked myself how it could be that a poetry which seemed in principle averse to complaint might nevertheless freely complain. Eliot despised complaint in the course of his pursuit of the classical, of a redemption from the personal, from the self, while Larkin might have been taken to be doing so in the course of an emergence from his romantic conditioning which left him poised, like the complaining A. E. Housman, between the classical and the romantic. Nevertheless, both Eliot and Larkin complain, and in neither case did I notice anything discrepant.

I failed to appreciate what it was for art to express self-pity, and what it was for art to dissemble, restrain or suspend it. Nor did I appreciate how powerful it can be, how resourceful, both in and out of art. I now believe that self-pity is too big a theme to be dealt with solely in terms of the discussion of adolescence and the need for it to cease, solely in terms of weakness and shame. It is there at the root of the artistic impulse, and of the individual life, and attempts at restraint should acknowledge this. It can be called a natural resource or native strength, and I have also known it to be called a virtue, one that enables you to feel something for other people. There is an implication here for the reader of Larkin's poetry, with its defect – or distinctive feature – of self-pity.

He once told someone that his inspiration lay in suffering: he was like the bird that can only sing when the thorn is at its breast. While this scarcely convicts him of the charge of self-pity, it does suggest that his poetry wouldn't have happened to a tougher guy. And yet Phil the Lark – Amis's name for him – was very tough, and so is his poetry. And other people love to read it. Too much, in other words, has been made of this 'defect'. But it is also true that too little has been made of it.

In referring to the vexed question of self-devotion in his work, I am not seeking to rephrase the 'English gentility' reproach that used to be levelled at Larkin. That is a different matter, and in any case something of a misconception. Nor do I think it cowardly of him, as one writer has claimed, to have experienced and given expression to his fears and disappointments. But I agree with Angela Carter that his work can make you feel that there must be more to life than this. (Had she known it, she would have enjoyed Francis Wyndham's rejoinder – that there were books that made him feel that there must be less to life than this.) Good poetry can make do with a limited range of subjects, and this is certainly the case with Larkin. But I can't think it ungrateful to make it a complaint about him that his range is narrow, for reasons that relate to the power and bias of a particular engagement with the self, and that it seems all the narrower for belonging to a poetry more openly autobiographical than Eliot's. Eliot complained in his verse, but it came as a surprise when he said so, when he spoke belatedly of the 'personal grumbling' in *The Waste Land*. It would have come as a greater surprise if Larkin had thought it necessary to say such a thing.

His *Selected Letters* of 1992 must have dismayed some, at least, of those of his admirers who had never wanted to see him as the modern master of self-pity. The romantic conditioning I have spoken of is exposed here, very interestingly: in the early days, Lawrence is tenderly discussed, and Dylan Thomas, in the flesh, is a 'hell of a fine chap'. But the unhappiness and unkindness of the letters were, for me, startling – accustomed though I had once been to treating letters as a form of diary, and as a first-rate complaining-place.

Put on, some of it, done to annoy; not to be taken seriously, some of it; excluded, almost all of it, from the poems he published, or transcended there. These things can be and have been said. But there is something to add. Self-division says unpleasant things, in the letters, about the black men to whose music he has thrilled; a 'rising tide of niggers' is flooding the country. As with Eliot, and with Evelyn Waugh, it isn't a strain to think of the exhibitions of snobbery and racism as the self-division of a suffering self-dislike, and it is right to take them seriously, just as it was presumably right to publish them. Of his old friend Kingsley Amis he writes towards the end of it all, in 1983: 'The only reason I hope I predecease him is that I'd find it next to impossible to say anything nice about him at his memorial service.' A joke, and no joke. A jealousy too. Reviewers of the collection were inclined to take for granted, in familiar fashion, a separation between the poet and the annoying persona to be seen in the letters (while also visible in some of the poems). Since then, the gap has been closed by those who have come forward to assign the poems, in bulk, to the persona. If this were the only way to close it, it would be better to let it yawn.

Dylan Thomas, deemed an arch-enemy by some members of the Movement, was, against the odds, a less confessional poet than Larkin. It isn't that he is classically impersonal, and he can even seem suicidal, in his letters and in the early poems which are his best.

> Before I knocked and flesh let enter,
> With liquid hands tapped on the womb . . .

When you start reading that poem, you scarcely know whether he wants to get out or to get in. But he was able none the less to disguise himself, to translate himself, in the exercise of his art, to avail himself, if you like, of the refuge and subterfuge of art. There are times when he can seem very like Drummond, who managed to be confessional even in his translations from other poets, but who also managed to leave behind a mystery as to what he was confessing. Damon and Dylan are rhetoricians of the self, pastoralists of the self, in Albany and on Fern Hill respectively, and in some degree dissemblers of their grief.

This, then, is the state I was in as my youth drew to its lingering close. I have tried to tell the story of a boy, of his engagements with himself, with friends, with books and their writers, while recognising that there have been plenty of other boys like me – like me, not least, in supposing themselves troubled and exceptional. I have been struck by coincidences between my actions and affiliations and those of my namesake Hugh Miller a hundred years before. He has the temerity to do as I have done and quote in his memoir from his adolescent poems, including a 'pasquinade' deriding one of his school-masters; a friend who wrote about his life, David Masson, was also to write the life of Drummond. And there is a good deal more of this. Not that I mean to scrape acquaintance with some full-blown alter ego. Hugh Miller's is a book which defies replicas – as it does the dissociation of sensibility from thought, of poetry from truth – and in which the writer never feels sorry for himself.

The 'Story of my Education' is laid before 'the working men of the country', in the hope of rousing them to 'the important work of self-culture and self-government' and of dissuading them from the 'numerous strikes' organised by tyrannical leaders. The country was Scotland, and Hugh Miller was a Scottish nationalist who was in favour of the union with England. His book describes the perseverance and apotheosis of the self-taught. Out of the chrysalis come the unruly boy, with his crustaceans, ammonites and magic caves, the mason, the naturalist and geologist, the editor, the self-made evangelistic Christian, the enemy in Church matters of landowners and the state at the time of the Disruption and the founding of the breakaway Free Kirk – away from those 'encroachments of the civil power' so little savoury to Jeanie Deans' father, douce Davie – and the writer who writes all this down in 'amenity of style', setting out his store of reflections, jokes and stories, of memorable and affecting human beings, like the woman who was sometimes mad and sometimes not, and who said to him: 'All your fellows are real masons; but you are merely in the disguise of a mason; and I have come to consult you about the deep matters of the soul.' She had seen through his working weeds, as my Cowgate crone had seen through mine.

The book ends when he sets out for Edinburgh to become an editor – 'a point at which, for the present, the story of my education must terminate'. At his house in Portobello, in 1856, two years after his book appeared, he shot himself with the loaded revolver he had taken to carrying about with him. He left behind him a note which speaks of excursions and transgressions in the night: 'I *must* have *walked*; and a fearful dream rises upon me. I cannot bear the horrible thought . . . My brain burns as the recollection grows.' He suffered from emphysema and silicosis, contracted during his work as a mason and as a researcher of his Old Red Sandstone; and he has also been thought, conjecturally, to have suffered from a brain tumour or from syphilis. He was superstitious, in Highland style, and had struggled with fearful and violent feelings. His efforts to make science of the seven days of creation, to overcome the idea of a continuous evolution, may have been part of his agony: what became Darwinian development had to be disproved. Miller held that man 'came into being *late on the Saturday evening*', and could look forward to a great Tomorrow, to the Sabbath of all time. Three years after his death the *Origin of Species* appeared.

The distresses of his last days are a deep matter of the soul, with their ancient resonances, their sense of the double life of a scientist who was also a night-walker. 'I felt as if I had been ridden by a witch for fifty miles.' The night before he died he read to his wife from the poem 'The Castaway' by William Cowper, his favourite poet, about a man whom God has rejected. The passage has the lines which I had once, coincidentally, applied to my father's death:

> he drank
> The stifling wave, and then he sank.

Superstition presents me with a further coincidence. Hugh Miller died two years after writing his life; two years after writing mine I shall be at the age at which my father died.

Suicide and superstition are features of this book which I did not anticipate when I began to write it, and there are other such features. I grew up in a world where authors and masters and traditions were desired and depended on, and I was a long time in becoming as sceptical of this dependency as I now think it advisable to be, while continuing to depend. In the book I have written there is more than I would have expected about class, to which this dependency relates in ways which were once hidden from me. I had understood myself to have neglected such matters when I was young, and relatively easy about the behaviour of those who have received, or who feel that they deserve, more money and more consideration than others: but it is more probable that I have cared about these matters, after my fashion, all along, so that what's said on the subject is, as it were, both early and late. I have also been taken aback, in remembering the kindness of friends and family, by the running contrast between gratitude and a sense of deprivation and hurt. Their kindness was to surround the spectacle – much of it staged in that theatre of the self constituted by the performances in my diaries – of a self-interest which cried out in pain.

There were some real pains among the pretended ones, and I put up with them, as people do, while fretting in their theatres; and I have since been no more fragile than the next person, though not silent either. I went on to exhibit brute purpose and passionate will in the shape of a Scots persistence, which has supplied the recitative for my coloratura desertions. I have worked hard, despite myself and in defiance of augury, which had me down in my youth as a wallower and a welterer, a Queen's Own Scottish Loiterer. Every so often, relatively uninteresting though it may be to confess it, I have even been thought stoical. There are opposites here which keep converging. Finding your courage, holding on, I have experienced as a duality and a drama, with self-pity listening to a voice which mentions other people's troubles, and urges me to try, as they try, to remain alive. I have no plan to commit suicide, and I don't imagine that any of this is uncommon.

I have made much of the strategies that anxiety and self-pity set going: the pre-emptive exaggeration, and so on. These might be termed poor man's bluff, and reckoned to incorporate the 'poor mouth' affected, at one time, in order to gain advantage or to remain alive, by the Irish poor; and they may also have owed a little to the art of complaint as practised by the Jews. They were accompanied by a taste for books in which I found them to be present, and I was later to find them to be present in books where they were, in a manner of speaking, proscribed. My own book has sometimes seemed to allege an escape from this welter. But I'd be inclined to exercise my scepticism about this, if I were me. There is, after all, the book itself to be conscious of, with its studious recall of these strategies. A superstitious habit of complaint, grief's histrionics, the serio-comedy of ominousness and netherness – they are still around. It may be that I am an example of the human doubleness predicated in romantic literature, whose witness in the matter I was to study and in some measure to believe. It may be that I am both stoical and morbid.

There is a definite morbidity in the contents of the room where I often sleep. Facing me as I lie in bed reading my books is the torso of, I think, a man. It's an anatomical model. His epidermis has been slit open, giving the appearance of a jacket. The ribs are laid bare and look like a waistcoat. Liver, lights, heart and lungs are on display, and he occasionally disembowels himself. Half his face is missing, and medicine has drawn the line at his genitals. My grandson visits him and calls him 'the poor man'. Over the man's head hangs the portrait of a youth who took his own life, together with an eighteenth-century print, a cross-section which shows women and boys slaving down below in Gilmerton pit. I like to lie, as if in my own coffin, amidst such memorabilia. They move me with their *memento mori*, their 'expect the worst'. I am that poor man. But then again I am not.

During the summer of 1992 I awoke in the country, in Dorset, to the sound of doves, having seen on television the night before a film of Alan Bennett's about a man who retires from work and soon dies. I found that I was composing a poem which imitated the sound of the doves.

> The infirm sad foreman,
> Such were his ways,
> Took early retirement
> At the end of his days.
>
> 'For my retirement
> Present,' his wife
> Was told, 'I fancy
> A silver knife.'
>
> 'Salvers are safer,'
> Replied his wife,
> 'And much less handy
> For ending life.'

The next day was my birthday. I recited my poem, and was later given the present of a silver paper-knife. It has a blade less sharp than the one my father took with him to his hospital.